COMPLETE

cocktails and finger f

COMPLETE cocktails and finger food

Elizabeth Wolf-Cohen and Oona van den Berg

LORENZ BOOKS

This edition published by Lorenz Books in 2001

Published in the USA by Lorenz Books
Anness Publishing Inc.
27 West 20th Street
New York
NY 10011

Lorenz Books is an imprint of Anness Publishing Inc.

www.lorenzbooks.com

Publisher: Joanna Lorenz
Managing Editor: Linda Fraser
Project Editor: Anne Hildyard
Designers: Alan Marshall and Eric Thompson
Photographers: Steve Baxter and Amanda Heywood
Stylist: Judy Williams

1 3 5 7 9 10 8 6 4 2

NOTES

Standard spoon and cup measures are level.

Large eggs are used unless otherwise stated.

A number of recipes in this book include raw egg.
Eggs have been known to carry Salmonella bacteria, which can cause severe and sometimes fatal poisoning.
Use only the freshest, best quality eggs and avoid using raw egg if you are very young,
old or have a compromised immune system

Contents

Fun Food & Canapes

A party is the perfect way to show off some of the prettiest and tastiest foods. And, because most of the preparation work can be done in advance, this kind of entertaining is generally much less demanding than formal dinner parties.

Planning the menu is the most enjoyable part of the preparations—informal or formal, large or small, close friends or business associates, the occasion will help you decide the right scale and approach. Time of day and the length of your guests' stay will also influence your arrangements—a few drinks with friends before going to a movie will require only one or two nibbles, whereas a three-hour party will obviously need something more substantial.

Small pieces of food that can be eaten with one hand make the best party foods (remember each guest will be holding a glass in one hand). Plan to have something to serve the moment people arrive, maybe a tray of crudités with a dip, as this gives guests something to focus on and helps them to relax. Move on to something hot when most people have arrived, then alternate between hot and cold, finishing with something warm or sweet. Serving sweet food is an ideal, subtle way of suggesting that the party is drawing to a close.

In this book, you will find easy recipes for simple roasted nuts and herbed olives, as well as more elaborate concoctions, such as wild rice pancakes with smoked salmon nests. But remember, with a little imagination almost any food can be adapted to party-sized pieces.

Condiments

Many different condiments can be used to put together a quick dip or snack at a moment's notice. Tomato ketchup and horseradish sauce can be stirred together with mayonnaise and a squeeze of lemon, to use as a dip for shrimp or hard-boiled eggs. Or, add chopped green onion to soy sauce and mango chutney and spoon onto Asian shrimp crackers for another instant snack. The variations are endless—just use your imagination.

Barbecue sauce
Bottled barbecue sauces are ideal for adding an outdoor flavor to broiled foods. They can be spread on pieces of meat or vegetables, which are then broiled and skewered onto toothpicks.

Capers
The little buds of the Mediterranean caper bush, preserved in vinegar, these add an extra piquancy to sauces and salads. They are especially good on pizzas and salads.

Chili sauce
This bottled sauce is widely available in supermarkets and Chinese grocers. It gives a warm sweet-spicy taste to most foods and sauces. Use in dips and marinades.

Corn relish
This sweet-and-tangy relish for hamburgers can also be used to top slices of cold chicken, beef, or ham, or hard-boiled eggs.

Dijon mustard
Indispensable for salad dressings, sauces, and dips, as well as to spread on meats and cheeses. It is sometimes flavored with green peppercorns or other aromatics.

English mustard
Sold already made up or as powder to be mixed to a paste. This is a traditional relish for accompanying beef, ham, and cheese.

Grainy mustard
The best known grainy mustard is from the region near Meaux, France, although other traditional whole-grain mustards are also available. It is delicious with ham and pâtés.

Horseradish sauce
This hot, spicy sauce can be bought as a relish, or "creamed" which makes it slightly milder. Often served with roast beef, it is also perfect with smoked and oily fish, chicken, and other seafood.

Mango chutney
Traditionally served with spicy food, this chutney is also delicious with cheese, ham, chicken mayonnaise, or egg salad.

Mayonnaise
A good-quality mayonnaise is indispensable. Use it as a dip or a spread, or to bind chopped hard-boiled eggs or chicken into toppings for toasts to serve as a quick canapé. Making your own is worth the effort.

Plum sauce
Made from plums, apricots, garlic, chilies, sugar, vinegar, and flavorings, this thick, sweet Cantonese condiment makes an ideal dip for Chinese-style snacks, or base for a barbecue sauce.

Soy sauce
This sauce is the basis of many Chinese-style dips and sauces. (Light soy sauce is more common than dark, but it is saltier, dilute it with a little water.) Add chopped green onions and cilantro for an easy dipping sauce.

Tartar sauce
This is the standard sauce for fried fish and shellfish. It is delicious with fish cakes. A mixture of mayonnaise, sweet gherkins, green onions, capers, and vinegar; try making your own.

Tomato chutney
Chutneys of all kinds make a tasty accompaniment to cold meats, savory pastries and salamis, as well as cheeses and cold broiled or grilled vegetables.

Tomato ketchup
This universal condiment can be used in barbecue sauces and marinades or spread on toast and topped with cheese or sliced meats for a quick canapé.

Herbs

Fresh herbs can be used generously in party foods, as they provide fresh flavor and interest to many different dishes. They also make a simple but elegant garnish. Use the same herb that you use in a recipe to garnish the serving plate—this provides a hint of what's in the food.

If you are lucky enough to have a garden, or even a window box, grow your own herbs so you will always have some to hand. If you can't grow your own, choose from the extensive range of fresh herbs available from supermarkets.

Basil
The warm, spicy scent of basil epitomizes the flavors of the Mediterranean. Use it with tomatoes, summer salads, vegetable dishes, and, of course, in pesto with pine nuts and Parmesan cheese.

Bay
This leaf of the laurel family gives a delicate flavor to soups, casseroles, and pâtés. Bay leaves make a pretty garnish which will stay fresh for hours.

Chives
A member of the onion family, the mild flavor is wonderful with almost anything, but especially in herb butters, cheeses, cream sauces, egg dishes, and, of course, with sour cream on baked potatoes.

Cilantro
This wonderfully aromatic herb is used in Mexican, Chinese, Indian, Greek, Turkish, and North African cooking, to add subtle spiciness to dishes such as stir-fries, curries, and hummus.

Dill
Most often used in fish dishes, such as the Scandinavian *gravlax*, the slightly aniseed flavor of dill is also delicious with eggs,potatoes, chicken, and cucumber, and in soft cheese recipes. Its soft, fernlike leaves make a lovely garnish.

Flat-leaf parsley
Sometimes called Italian parsley, this variety has a slightly stronger flavor than curly parsley. It adds interest and color to almost any savory dish, especially vegetables and fish, and makes a beautiful garnish.

Lemongrass
The stem of this lemon-scented broad-leaved grass is used in Southeast Asian dishes, especially those from Thailand. If you cannot find it, substitute a little freshly grated lemon peel.

Mint
This herb, with its many varieties, gives a fresh tingle to fish, goat cheeses, and salads, and is wonderful in dips. It is used extensively in Middle Eastern cooking.

Oregano
Sometimes called wild majoram, this has a powerful flavor used in tomato sauces and with vegetable dishes of the southern Mediterranean and Greece.

Thyme
This intensely aromatic herb is used in lamb or chicken dishes. It is also good in tomato sauces and vegetable dishes, and is an integral part of a bouquet garni.

Watercress
Technically, this is a vegetable and a member of the mustard family. Its peppery flavor is particularly good in sandwiches or with egg and fish, and it can be used as an attractive garnish.

Kitchen Cupboard Nibbles

It is always a good idea to keep a variety of nuts and other nibbles in the cupboard. Often a few potato chips, peanuts, or olives are all you need to offer with drinks before going out or before a meal. Look in specialty gourmet stores and ethnic markets for unusual nibbles.

Bread sticks (grisşini)
Stand these in a pitcher for an easy snack on their own or with something to dip into, or spread each with a little herb butter.

Bombay mix
Commercially prepared versions of this Indian snack are sold in Asian grocery stores. It is a mixture of fried nuts, legumes, and other nibbles flavored with curry spices—perfect before an Indian meal.

Cheese straws
These cheese-flavored twists of flaky pastry look pretty and make a tasty snack.

Dried apricots
Dried fruit makes an interesting alternative to salty, savory nibbles. Also, try dried peaches, dates, prunes, figs, and banana chips for healthy snacks.

Dried cranberries
Popular as a baking ingredient, these are also good on their own or mixed with dried cherries.

Gherkins
Little sweet pickled gherkins are delicious as an appetizer, as well as being low in calories.

Green olives
A wide variety of olives is available in supermarkets. For a party snack, the pitted variety are the most convenient. Spanish olives are often stuffed with tiny pieces of red pimiento, almonds, or anchovies.

Honey roast cashews
These biscuit-flavored nuts have a slightly sweet, honey coating.

Japanese rice crackers
These puffs of rice with peanuts inside or wrapped with dried seaweed, these make a sophisticated nibble and look very attractive.

Macadamia nuts
These nuts come from Hawaii and Australia and have a delicate, slightly sweet flavor. They are expensive but delicious.

Pistachio nuts
Always popular these pretty green nuts are sold still in their shells. Don't forget to provide little dishes for the empty shells.

Pita chips
These tiangles of pita bread brushed with oil and sprinkled with herbs, and baked until crisp and golden, provide a crunchy snack.

Popcorn
Plain popcorn makes a healthy, low-calorie snack. Tossed with butter or oil and salt, it is even more delicious, but more calorific. Various flavors of popped corn can be found in most supermarkets.

Potato chips
Universally popular, chips come in a bewildering variety of flavors.

Pretzel sticks
A delicious crunchy snack, these salty sticks are handy to keep as a standby, and easy to serve.

Shrimp crackers
These commercially-made pale puffs are crunchy and scented with a shrimp flavor. They are often served in Chinese or Thai restaurants.

Tortilla chips
Triangles of fried corn, these little tortillas are ideal with a drink or cocktail such as a margarita. They are also sold with chili flavoring.

shrimp crackers

Japanese rice crackers

popcorn

macadamia nuts

cheese straws
tortilla chips
pita crisps
dried apricots
Bombay mix
gherkins
green olives
pistachios
dried cranberries
potato crisps
bread sticks (grissini)
pretzel sticks
honey roast cashews

Garnishes

Garnishes on party food need to last longer than those on a dinner plate, which are eaten immediately—so keep them simple. Green, yellow, and red tend to bring out the color in foods, so stick to what looks best.

LEMON/CUCUMBER TWISTS

1 With a canelle knife, remove strips of peel down the length of the lemon or cucumber. Slice thinly, then make a slit from one edge to the center of each slice.

2 Twist the sides in opposite directions to form a twist.

RADISH FANS

1 Using a sharp knife, cut lengthwise slits, leaving the stem end intact.

2 Gently push the radish to one side, causing the slices to fan out.

CHILI FLOWERS

1 Slit the chilies lengthwise and gently scrape out any seeds. Cut lengthwise into as many strips as possible, leaving the stem ends intact.

2 Drop the chilies into a bowl of iced water and refrigerate several hours until curled. (The iced water causes the strips to curl back.)

GREEN ONION POMPOMS

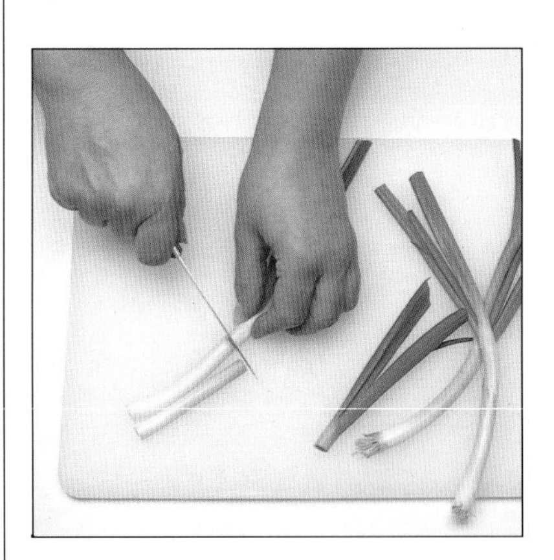

1 Trim the green onions and cut each into pieces about 3 inches long.

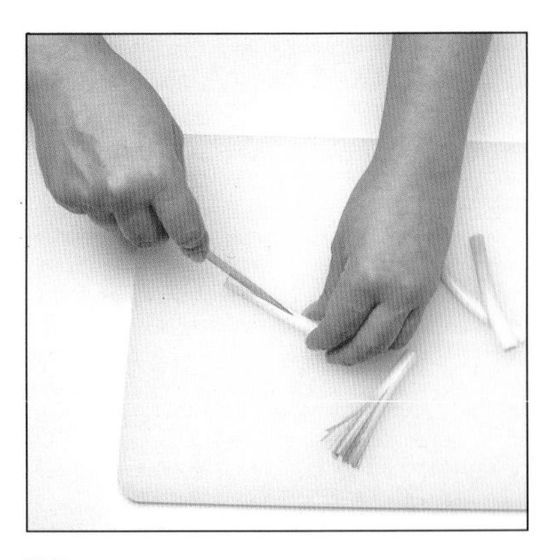

2 Using a small knife, cut as many slits lengthwise as possible, leaving the root end intact. Drop into a bowl of iced water and refrigerate for several hours or overnight until curled. (The iced water causes the strips to curl back.)

Cutting Carrot Julienne

It may seem a little time-consuming and fiddly to cut vegetables into thin julienne strips, but the result is definitely worth it.

1 Peel a carrot and take a thin slice off each side to square it up. Cut into 5 cm/2 in lengths.

2 Cut each of the lengths into 5 mm/¼ in thick slices.

3 Stack the slices and cut these into fine matchsticks to form julienne.

Making a Radish Rose

This is a classic garnish. The technique can also be applied to the bulb of a salad onion or a baby turnip. Radish roses can be made in advance and kept in water in the fridge for up to 3 days.

1 Carefully trim both ends of the radish, removing the root and stalk.

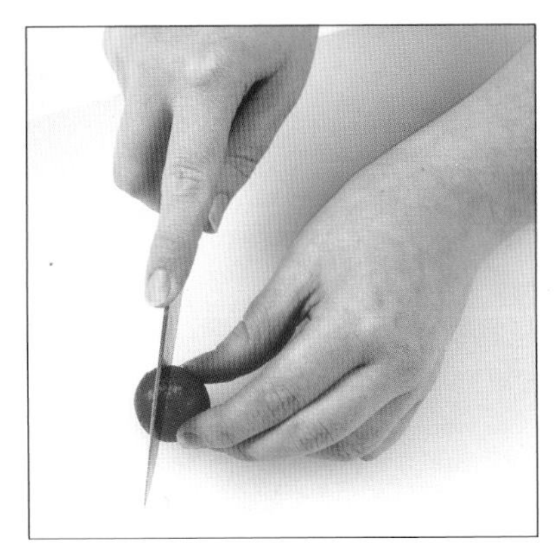

2 Place base-end down and cut in half vertically, stopping the knife just before it reaches the base. Repeat until the radish looks as though it has been cut into eight equal segments, but is in fact held together at the base.

3 Put the radish in a bowl of iced water and leave for at least 4 hours to open up.

Blanching

Blanching is a method of partial cooking, where foods are immersed in boiling water or boiled briefly. In terms of garnishing, the technique is used to make vegetables, fruit or herbs more pliable and easier to handle. It also helps to preserve a bright colour.

1 Fill a large saucepan with water and bring to the boil. Add the prepared vegetable or fruit for the time suggested in each individual recipe: 1–2 minutes is usually ample.

2 Drain well in a colander, then refresh in cold water. Change the water once or twice, as necessary, until the food is completely cold. Drain again.

3 Blanched vegetables and fruit can be used in various ways: stamped out into diamonds, perhaps, or tied in a bundle with a wilted chive.

Peeling Tomatoes

It only takes a few moments to peel tomatoes, but the difference this makes to a dish is amazing. Concassing tomatoes (chopping them into neat squares) adds the finishing touch.

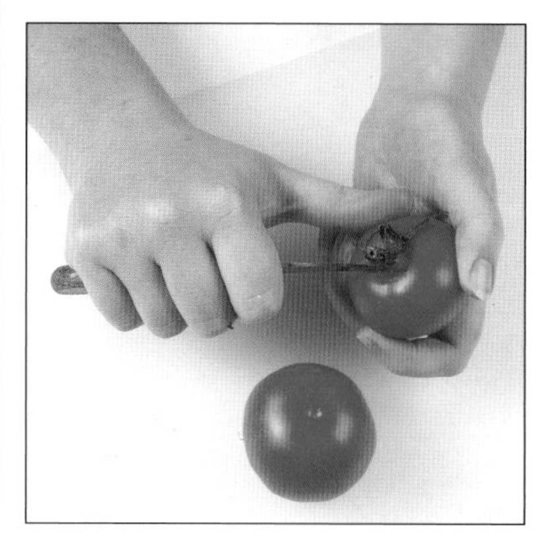

1 Make a small cross in the skin on the base of each tomato. Use a small sharp knife to cut out the calyx.

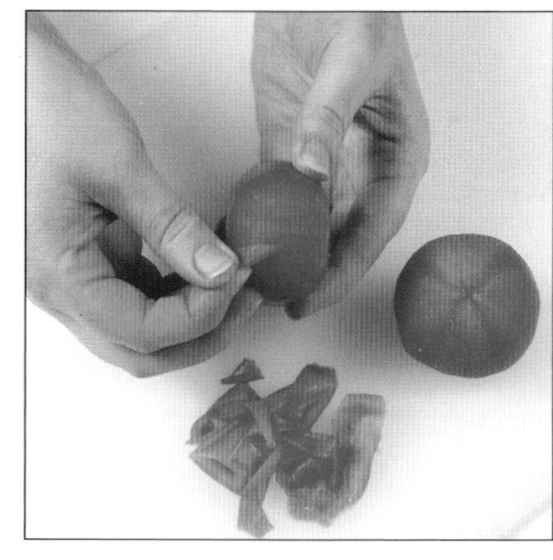

2 Place the tomatoes in boiling water for 20–30 seconds, drain and refresh under cold water. Gently peel off the loosened skin.

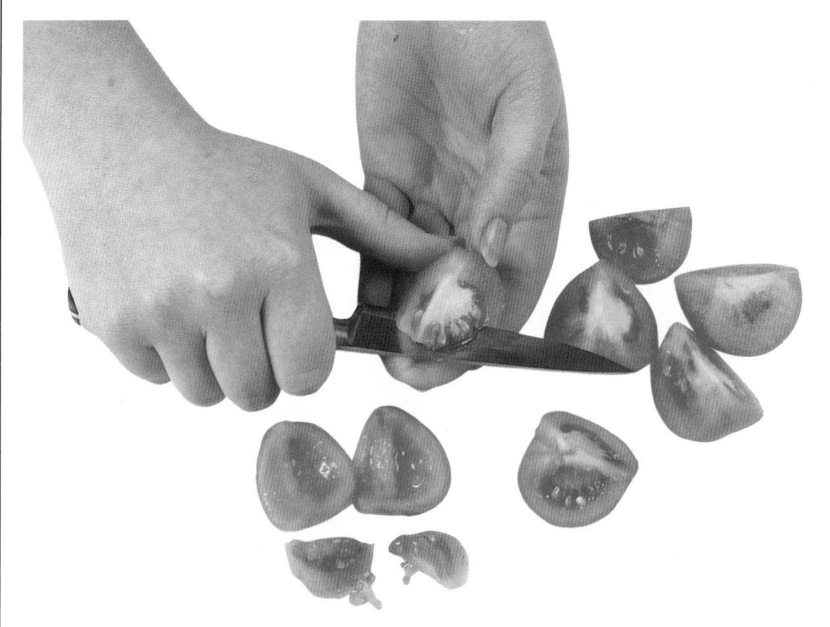

3 Cut the tomatoes into quarters. Place each tomato quarter flesh-side down and slide a knife along the inner flesh, scooping out all the seeds. Cut the flesh into neat 5 mm/¼ in squares.

Roasting Sweet Peppers

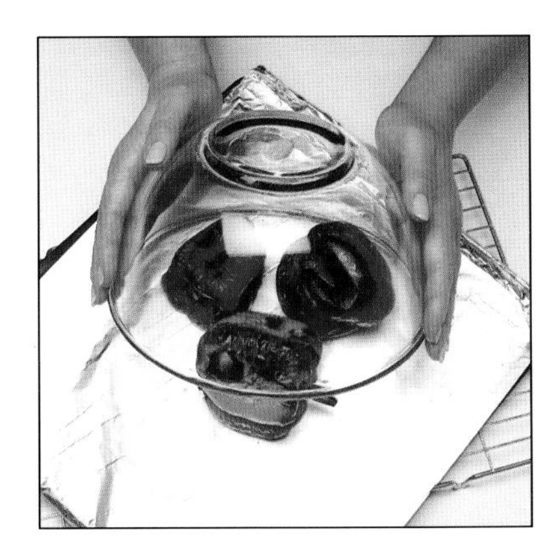

1 Place the peppers on a foil-lined baking sheet and grill until blackened and blistered on all sides, turning occasionally. Cover the peppers with a large bowl or place in a plastic bag and seal, until cool.

2 Using a sharp knife, peel off the charred skin. Cut the peppers into strips, removing the core and seeds but reserving any juices.

Lining Small Tartlet Tins

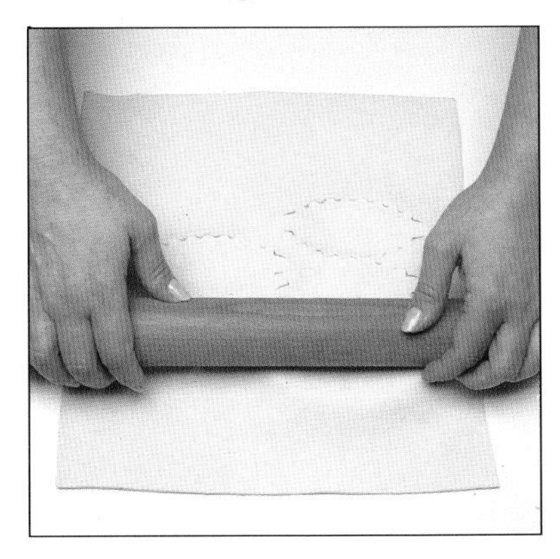

1 Roll out the dough as the recipe directs. Arrange the tartlet tins close to each other on a work surface. Roll the dough loosely back on to the rolling pin then roll out over the tins. Roll the rolling pin firmly over the dough to cut the edges.

2 Using both thumbs, carefully press the dough into the bottom and up the sides of the tins.

Using a Canelle Knife

1 Holding the fruit or vegetable in one hand, pull the canelle knife along the surface at regular intervals to create grooves in the surface.

2 Cut the fruit or vegetable horizontally to make pretty, ridged slices.

Easy Sauces and Spreads

MAYONNAISE

Homemade mayonnaise is well worth making to use as a spread or dip. If you like, add some herbs along with the egg yolks. Remember mayonnaise is made with raw egg yolks, so use fresh eggs from a good supplier. Raw eggs are not suitable for young children, the elderly, or pregnant women.

Makes about 1½ cups

INGREDIENTS
2 egg yolks
1 tablespoon Dijon mustard
1 tablespoon white wine vinegar
1¼ cups olive oil or half olive oil and half sunflower oil

1 Put the egg yolks in the bowl of a food processor. Add the mustard and vinegar and process for 10 seconds to blend.

2 With the machine running, gradually pour the oil through the feed tube until a smooth paste forms. Pour into a jar and spoon a little more oil over to seal the surface. Cover tightly and refrigerate, where it will keep for up to one week, or freeze in smaller quantities.

EASY PESTO SAUCE

Pesto is a delicious sauce which can be used on its own or stirred into sour cream or mayonnaise to make a quick dip. Use a good-quality olive oil.

Makes about 1¼ cups

INGREDIENTS
about 2 cups fresh basil leaves
1 to 2 garlic cloves
3 tablespoons freshly grated Parmesan cheese
3 tablespoons pine nuts, lightly toasted
salt
freshly ground black pepper
4 to 6 tablespoons virgin olive oil, plus extra for sealing

1 Put the basil leaves, garlic, Parmesan cheese, and pine nuts in the bowl of a food processor. Season with salt and pepper and process until well blended, scraping down the side of the bowl once or twice.

2 With the machine running, gradually pour the oil through the feed tube in a steady stream until all the oil is incorporated and the sauce is thickened. Add 1 to 2 tablespoons boiling water and process briefly to blend. Will keep in the refrigerator for up to 3 days.

QUICK TAPENADE

Tapenade is an olive spread served in the Mediterranean as a tasty snack spread on toasts, or stirred into soups and stews. Keep it on hand for quick *crostini* or stir into soft cheese for an easy spread or dip.

Makes about 1 cup

INGREDIENTS
- 2/3 cup kalamata, or other oil-cured ripe olives, pitted
- 1 to 2 garlic cloves
- 1 tablespoon capers, rinsed and drained
- 3 tablespoons virgin olive oil, plus extra for sealing
- 2 to 4 anchovy fillets, drained
- juice of 1/2 lemon
- chopped fresh cilantro

1 Put all the ingredients, except the cilantro into the bowl of a food processor and process until finely chopped, scraping down the side of the bowl once or twice.

2 Spoon into a small bowl and stir in the chopped cilantro. Spoon a little extra olive oil over to seal. Cover and refrigerate up to 2 weeks.

BASIC TOMATO SAUCE

This sauce can be used as the base for pasta or vegetable sauces, as a pizza base, or a seasoned dip. Use ripe tomatoes with lots of flavor and your favorite herbs.

Makes about 1 1/3 cups

INGREDIENTS
- 2 tablespoons olive oil
- 1 large onion, chopped
- 1 to 2 garlic cloves, chopped
- 1/2 teaspoon chopped fresh thyme leaves or 1/4 teaspoon dried thyme
- 1 to 2 bay leaves
- 6 to 8 ripe plum tomatoes
- 1/4 cup water or stock
- 1 to 2 teaspoons chopped fresh herbs

1 In a large skillet or saucepan, heat the olive oil over medium heat. Add the onions and cook for 5 to 7 minutes, stirring frequently, until softened. Add the garlic, thyme, and bay leaves and cook for 1 minute longer. Stir in the tomatoes and water or stock. Bring to a boil and cook, uncovered, for 15 to 20 minutes over medium heat until most of the liquid has evaporated and the sauce has thickened.

2 Pour into the bowl of a food processor and process until smooth. Press through a strainer to remove any skin and seeds, then stir in the herbs. Cool and refrigerate for up to 4 days.

Hot Pepper Pecans

These nuts are easy to make and can be prepared up to a week ahead, then stored in an airtight container.

Makes about 3 cups

INGREDIENTS
- 1 tablespoon butter
- 1 tablespoon sesame oil
- 3 cups pecan halves
- 1 to 2 tablespoons soy sauce
- 2 to 3 dashes hot-pepper sauce, or to taste
- 1 tablespoon clear honey (optional)

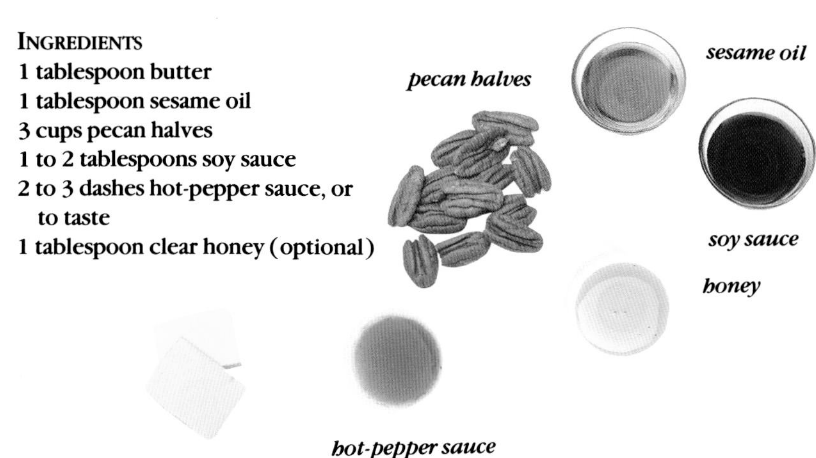

1 Preheat the oven to 300°F. Put the butter and oil on a medium-size baking tray and heat in the oven until the butter melts. Remove and swirl to blend. Stir in the pecans until well coated, then toast them in the oven for 30 minutes, stirring once or twice.

2 Sprinkle the soy sauce over the nuts, then add a few dashes of hot-pepper sauce and the honey, if using. Toss the nuts until well coated, then allow to cool. Store in an airtight container.

Easy Nachos

This Tex-Mex specialty, a spicy cheese snack that can be made in minutes, is always popular.

Makes 24

INGREDIENTS
- 2 or 3 fresh or pickled jalapeño or other medium-hot chili peppers
- 24 large tortilla chips
- scant 2 cups grated Cheddar cheese
- 2 green onions, finely chopped
- sour cream, to serve (optional)

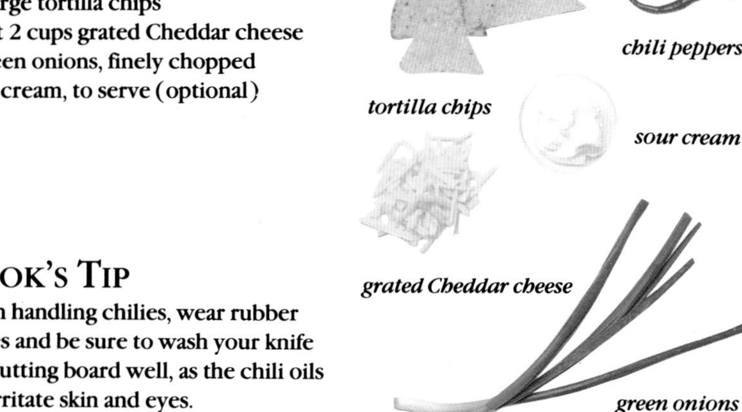

COOK'S TIP

When handling chilies, wear rubber gloves and be sure to wash your knife and cutting board well, as the chili oils can irritate skin and eyes.

1 With a small sharp knife, split the chili peppers and remove the seeds (the hottest part). Slice thinly.

2 Preheat the oven to 425°F. Arrange the tortilla chips in a single layer on a large baking tray lined with foil. Sprinkle a little grated cheese onto each tortilla chip and top with a slice of chili and a few green onions. Bake for about 5 minutes until golden and bubbling. Serve hot with sour cream, if you like.

Spicy Microwave Poppadums

This is a wonderfully easy way to prepare a spicy snack. Poppadums are Indian and traditionally fried, but this method is much lighter.

Makes 6 or 12

INGREDIENTS
6 poppadums, broken in half if you wish
vegetable oil for brushing
cayenne pepper or chili powder

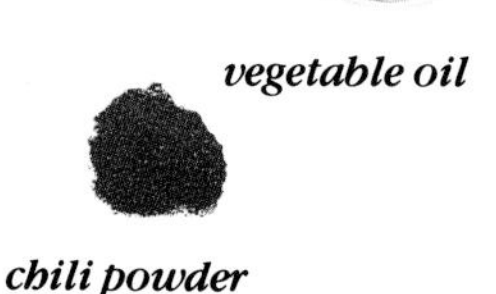

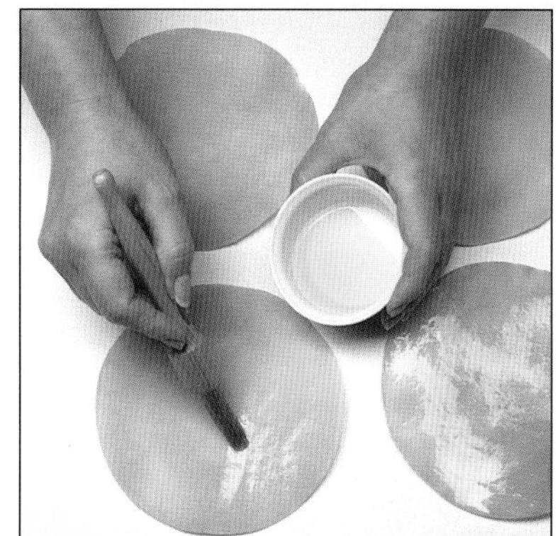

1 Lay the poppadums on a counter and brush each one lightly with a little vegetable oil. Sprinkle with a pinch of cayenne pepper or chili powder.

2 Arrange 2 to 4 poppadums (depending on the size of your microwave) on paper towels and microwave on High (100%) for 40 to 60 seconds. Serve immediately.

VARIATION

If you don't have a microwave, you can make the same snack by using poppadums which can be broiled, and following the directions on the package after step one. Look for boxes of flat poppadums in Asian grocery stores.

Hot-and-Spicy Popcorn

This is an ideal nibble for a crowd. Making your own popcorn is easy, but you can use the popped, store-bought variety if you like. Adjust the chili powder to suit your taste.

Makes about 12 cups

INGREDIENTS
½ cup vegetable oil, plus extra for popping
1 cup unpopped popcorn
2 to 3 garlic cloves, crushed
1 to 2 teaspoons chili powder (according to taste)
pinch cayenne pepper
salt

1 In a large heavy saucepan, heat the extra oil, then pop the corn according to the manufacturer's directions.

2 In a small saucepan, combine the oil, the garlic cloves, chili powder, and cayenne pepper. Cook over low heat for about 5 minutes, stirring occasionally. Remove the garlic cloves with a slotted spoon, then pour the flavored oil over the popped popcorn. Toss well to combine and season with salt to taste. Serve warm or at room temperature.

VARIATION

For Parmesan Popcorn, omit the chili powder and salt and proceed as above. After pouring over the seasoned oil, add 4 to 6 tablespoons freshly grated Parmesan cheese, and toss well.

Celery Sticks with Roquefort

This delicious filling can also be made with English Stilton or any other blue cheese. Diluted with a little milk or cream, it also makes a delicious dip.

Makes about 45

INGREDIENTS
- 7 ounces Roquefort or other blue cheese, softened
- 1¼ cups lowfat cream cheese
- 2 green onions, finely chopped
- black pepper
- 1 to 2 tablespoons milk
- 1 celery head
- chopped walnuts or hazelnuts, to garnish

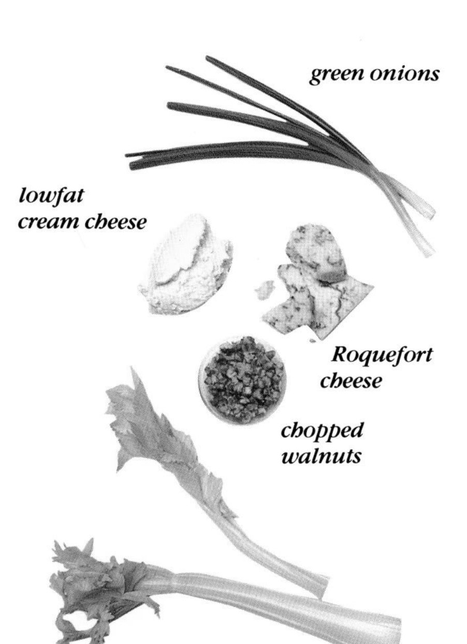

1 With a fork, crumble the Roquefort in a bowl. Put in a food processor with the cream cheese, green onions, and black pepper. Process until smooth, scraping down the side of the bowl once or twice and gradually adding milk if the mixture seems too stiff.

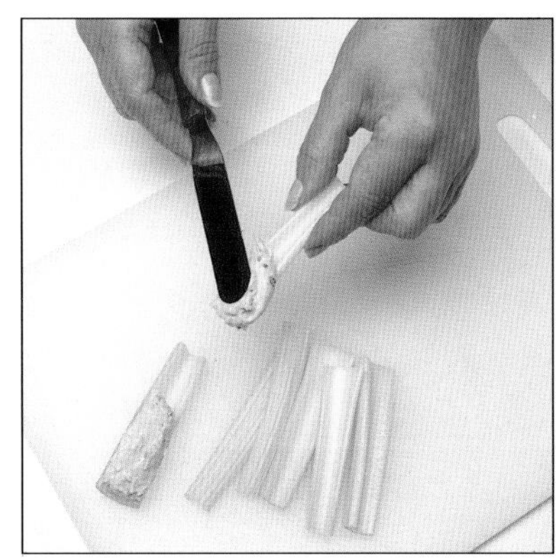

2 If you like, peel the celery lightly to remove any heavy strings before cutting each stalk into 3- to 4-inch pieces. Using a small knife, fill each celery stick with a little cheese mixture and press on a few chopped nuts. Arrange on a serving plate and refrigerate until ready to serve.

COOK'S TIP

For a more elegant presentation, fill a pastry bag fitted with a small star tip with the cheese mixture and carefully pipe mixture into the celery sticks. Press on the nuts.

Italian-style Marinated Artichokes

Good-quality extra-virgin olive oil together with fresh herbs, turn canned or frozen artichoke hearts into a delicious snack.

Makes about 3 cups

INGREDIENTS
- 2 × 14-ounce cans artichoke hearts in salt water
- ¾ cup extra-virgin olive oil
- 1 teaspoon chopped fresh thyme, or ½ teaspoon dried thyme
- 1 teaspoon chopped fresh oregano or marjoram, or ½ teaspoon dried oregano or marjoram
- ½ teaspoon fennel seeds, lightly crushed
- 1 to 2 garlic cloves, finely chopped
- freshly ground black pepper
- grated peel and juice of ½ lemon

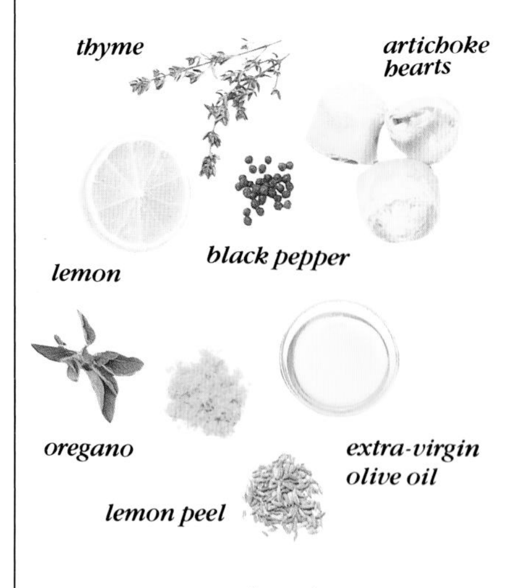

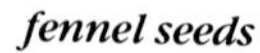

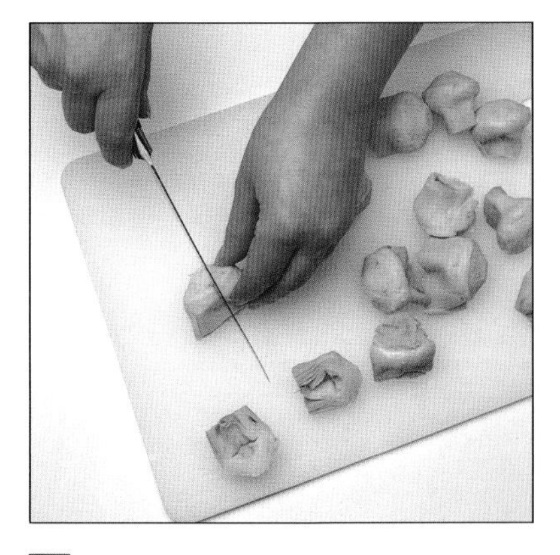

1 Rinse the artichokes, then drain them on paper towels. Cut any large ones in half lengthwise.

2 Put the artichokes in a large saucepan with the next six ingredients, stir to combine, then cook, covered, over very low heat for 8 to 10 minutes until the flavors infuse. Remove from the heat and leave to cool slightly, then gently stir in the lemon peel and juice. Refrigerate. Return to room temperature before serving on toothpicks.

Prosciutto Grissini

This is an easy way to combine two well-loved ingredients for a quick nibble with no real cooking.

Makes about 24

Ingredients
8 ounces prosciutto, very thinly sliced
1 × 4-ounce box grissini (Italian bread sticks)
basil leaves, to garnish (optional)

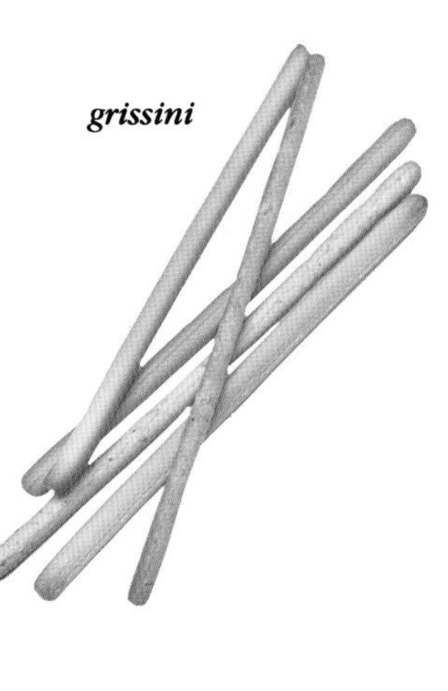

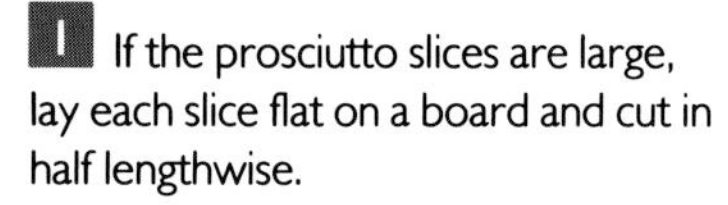

1 If the prosciutto slices are large, lay each slice flat on a board and cut in half lengthwise.

2 Wrap each bread stick with a half-slice of prosciutto, tucking in a basil leaf if you like, to come half way down the bread stick. Arrange on a plate and cover until ready to serve. Garnish with fresh basil if you like.

Cook's Tip

Do not prepare too far in advance as the moisture from the ham will cause the bread sticks to bend.

Variation

Substitute half slices of thinly smoked salmon and garnish with sprigs of dill instead of basil.

Aromatic Greek Olives with Feta

Prepare lots of these and store them in the refrigerator for unexpected guests. They will keep for about a month in a tightly closed container, but remember to bring them to room temperature before serving.

Makes 3 cups

Ingredients
¾ cup virgin olive oil
1 tablespoon cumin seeds, lightly crushed
1 tablespoon coriander seeds, lightly crushed
1 tablespoon fennel seeds, lightly crushed
1 teaspoon cardamom pods, crushed
½ teaspoon crushed red-pepper flakes
¼ teaspoon ground cinnamon
4 to 6 garlic cloves, crushed
grated peel and juice of 1 lemon
3 cups kalamata or other oil-cured olives, drained

To serve
8 ounces feta cheese, cut into ½-inch cubes
1 to 2 tablespoons virgin olive oil
freshly ground black pepper
1 to 2 tablespoons chopped fresh cilantro or parsley

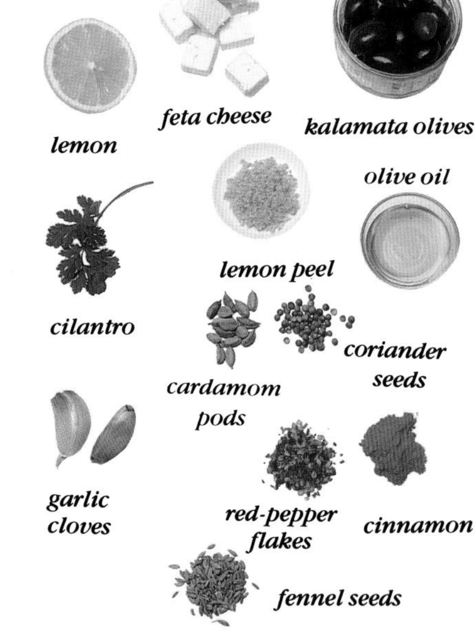

1 In a medium-size saucepan, combine the olive oil, spices, and garlic. Cook over medium-low heat for 3 to 5 minutes until warm and fragrant, stirring occasionally.

COOK'S TIP

The seasoned feta cheese cubes make a delicious nibble on their own.

2 Remove the pan from the heat and stir in the lemon peel and juice, then add the olives, tossing until well combined, set aside to cool. Transfer to an airtight container or jar to refrigerate.

3 Bring the olives to room temperature, pour in to a bowl. Put the feta cubes in another bowl, drizzle the olive oil over, and season with black pepper, then sprinkle with chopped cilantro or parsley. Serve the olives with the cheese cubes.

Parmesan Phyllo Triangles

You can whip up these light and crunchy triangles at the last minute using fresh or frozen sheets of phyllo pastry.

Makes about 24

INGREDIENTS
3 large sheets phyllo pastry
olive oil, for brushing
3 to 4 tablespoons freshly grated Parmesan cheese
½ teaspoon crumbled dried thyme or sage

1 Preheat the oven to 350°F. Line a large cookie sheet with foil and brush lightly with oil. Lay one sheet of phyllo pastry on a counter and brush lightly with a little olive oil. Sprinkle lightly with half the Parmesan and a little dried thyme or sage. Cover with a second sheet of phyllo, brush with a little more oil, and sprinkle with the remaining cheese and thyme or sage. Top with the remaining sheets of phyllo and brush very lightly with a little more oil.

2 With a sharp knife, cut the phyllo pastry stack in half lengthwise and then into squares. Cut each square into triangles.

3 Arrange the triangles on the cookie sheet, scrunching them slightly. Do not allow them to touch. Bake for 6 to 8 minutes until crisp and golden. Cool slightly and serve.

COOK'S TIP

These will keep in an airtight container for up to three days, but handle carefully as they are very fragile. Reheat in a medium oven to crisp when you are ready to serve them.

Nutty Cheese Balls

These tasty morsels are perfect for nibbling with drinks.

Makes 32

INGREDIENTS
4 oz cream cheese
4 oz Roquefort cheese
1 cup finely chopped walnuts
chopped fresh parsley, to coat
paprika, to coat
salt and freshly ground black pepper

1 Beat the two cheeses together until smooth using an electric beater.

2 Stir in the chopped walnuts and season with salt and pepper.

3 Shape into small balls (about a rounded teaspoonful each). Chill on a baking sheet until firm.

4 Roll half the balls in the chopped parsley and half in the paprika. Serve on toothpicks.

Salami and Olive Cheese Wedges

Genoa salami is delicious with the olives.

Makes 24

INGREDIENTS
8 oz cream cheese
1 tsp paprika
½ tsp English mustard powder
2 tbsp stuffed green olives, chopped
8 oz sliced salami
sliced olives, to garnish

1 Beat the cream cheese with the paprika and mustard and mix well. Stir in the chopped olives.

2 Spread the salami slices with the olive mixture and stack five slices on top of each other. Wrap in plastic wrap and chill until firm. With a sharp knife, cut each stack into four wedges. Garnish with additional sliced olives and serve with a toothpick through each wedge, to hold the slices together.

Cheese and Pesto Pastries

These pastries can be made ahead and frozen uncooked. Freeze them in a single layer and then transfer them to a freezer-proof container. To serve, arrange the pastries on baking trays, brush them with oil and bake from frozen for 5–10 minutes longer than the recommended time.

Serves 8

INGREDIENTS
8 oz frozen chopped spinach
2 tbsp pine nuts
4 tbsp pesto sauce
4 oz Gruyère cheese
½ cup grated Parmesan cheese
2 × 10 oz packet of frozen filo pastry, thawed
2 tbsp olive oil
salt and freshly ground black pepper, to taste

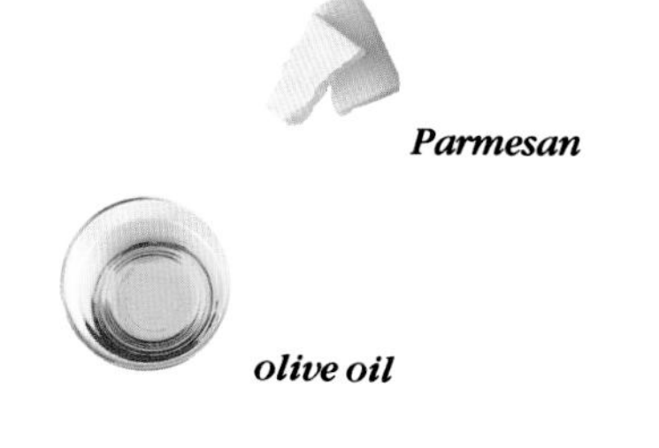

Parmesan

olive oil

spinach

pesto sauce

filo pastry

pine nuts

1 Preheat the oven to 375°F. Prepare the filling; put the frozen spinach into a pan, and heat gently, breaking it up as it defrosts. Increase the heat to evaporate any excess moisture. Transfer to a bowl and cool slightly.

2 Put the pine nuts into a frying pan and stir over a very low heat until they are lightly toasted. Chop them and add them to the spinach, with the pesto and Gruyère and Parmesan cheeses. Season to taste.

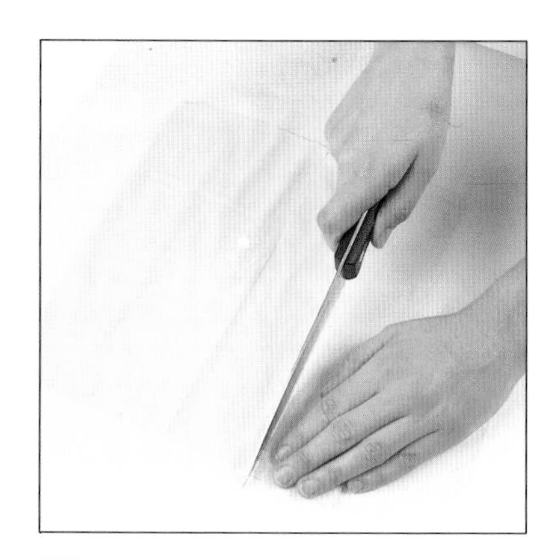

3 Unwrap the filo pastry and cover it with plastic wrap and a damp dish towel (to prevent it from drying out). Take one sheet at a time and cut it into 2 in wide strips. Brush each strip with oil.

4 Put a teaspoon of filling on one end of each strip of pastry. Fold the end over in a triangle, enclosing the filling.

5 Continue to fold the triangle over and over again until the end of the strip is reached. Repeat with the other strips, until all the filling has been used up.

6 Place the pastries on baking trays, brush them with oil and bake for 20–25 minutes, or until golden brown. Cool on a wire rack. Serve warm.

Spiced Mixed Nuts

Spices are a delicious addition to mixed roasted nuts.

Makes 2 cups

INGREDIENTS
⅔ cup brazil nuts
⅔ cup cashew nuts
⅔ cup almonds
1 tsp garam masala
½ tsp ground coriander
½ tsp salt
2 tbsp butter, melted

1 Preheat the oven to 350°F. Put all the nuts and spices and the salt on to a baking tray and mix well.

2 Pour the melted butter over and bake for 10–15 minutes, stirring until golden brown.

3 Drain on paper towels and allow to cool before serving.

Herby Cheese Crackers

Use a selection of festive shapes for cutting out these crackers.

Makes 32

INGREDIENTS
3 cups all-purpose flour
½ tsp cayenne pepper
1 tsp English mustard powder
¾ cup butter
6 oz sharp Cheddar cheese, grated finely
1 tbsp mixed dried herbs
1 egg, beaten
salt and freshly ground black pepper

1 Preheat the oven to 400°F. Sift the flour, cayenne pepper and mustard powder together into a bowl or food processor.

2 Rub the butter into the flour and add the cheese, herbs and seasoning. Stir in the beaten egg to bind, and knead to a smooth dough.

3 On a lightly floured work surface, roll the dough out thinly. Stamp it into small biscuits with cutters. Bake for 10–15 minutes, or until golden. Cool on a wire rack. Store in an airtight container.

Mini Macaroons

Try these chewy macaroons with a glass of wine —in France, sweet cookies are often served with Champagne.

Makes about 34

INGREDIENTS
1¼ cups blanched almonds
⅔ cup + 1 tablespoon sugar
2 egg whites
½ teaspoon almond or natural vanilla extract
confectioners' sugar, for dusting (optional)

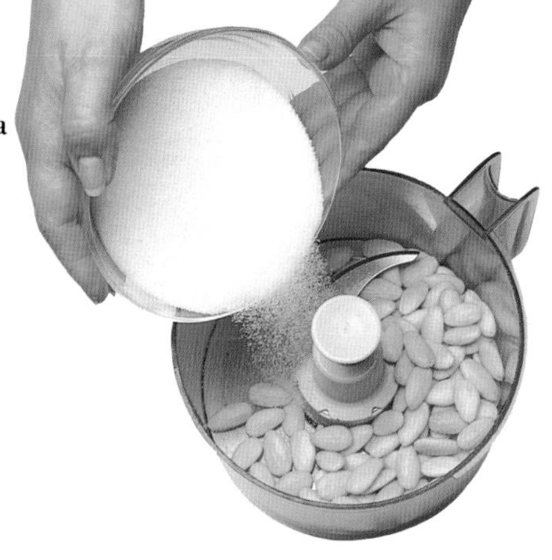

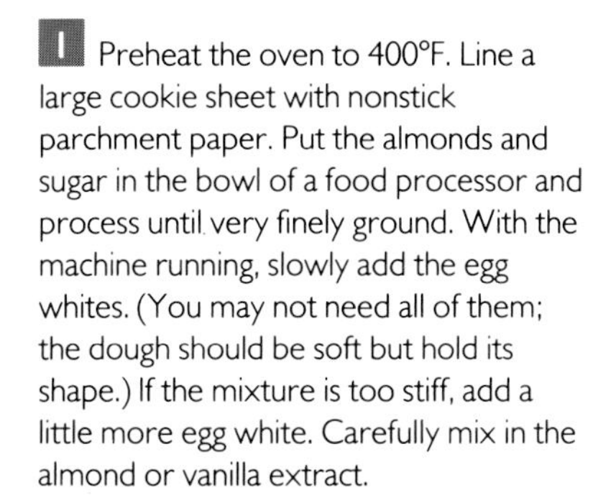

1 Preheat the oven to 400°F. Line a large cookie sheet with nonstick parchment paper. Put the almonds and sugar in the bowl of a food processor and process until very finely ground. With the machine running, slowly add the egg whites. (You may not need all of them; the dough should be soft but hold its shape.) If the mixture is too stiff, add a little more egg white. Carefully mix in the almond or vanilla extract.

2 With moistened hands, shape the mixture into about 34 small balls and arrange on the cookie sheet about 1½ inches apart. With the back of a wet spoon, flatten the tops and dust them lightly with confectioners' sugar.

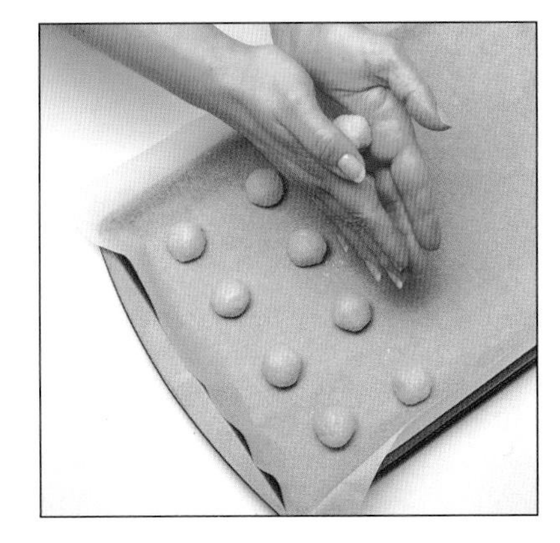

3 Bake for 12 to 15 minutes until the tops just begin to color and the macaroons feel slightly firm. Transfer the cookie sheet to a wire rack to cool, dust with more confectioners' sugar if you like, then remove the macaroons from the paper.

VARIATION

If you like, press an extra blanched almond half on top of each macaroon before baking.

Crudités and Dips

Dips and their accompanying raw vegetables—crudités—seem to be an inevitable feature of any informal gathering, because they are such ideal party food. Just about anything can be included in the crudité category—asparagus spears, zucchini, other raw or blanched vegetables, strips of cheese, melon, cooked chicken . . . all these can be dipped into a variety of mixtures that come from around the world—guacamole from Mexico, hummus and taramasalata from Greece, sweet mustard sauce from Sweden, spicy dhal from India, olivada from Spain, or tapenade from France. The following two dips are easy to make and can be prepared at the last minute.

Slicing Peppers

1 Cut off the bottom of the pepper and stand the pepper on the cut edge. Cut down each side of the core to obtain 4 flat sides.

2 Cut each side into triangular-shaped spears to serve as crudités.

Easy Oriental Dip

Makes about 1 cup

INGREDIENTS
½ cup sunflower oil
¼ cup toasted sesame oil
1-inch piece fresh gingerroot, peeled
1 to 2 garlic cloves, crushed
2 green onions, finely chopped
1 small red chili, seeds removed, finely chopped

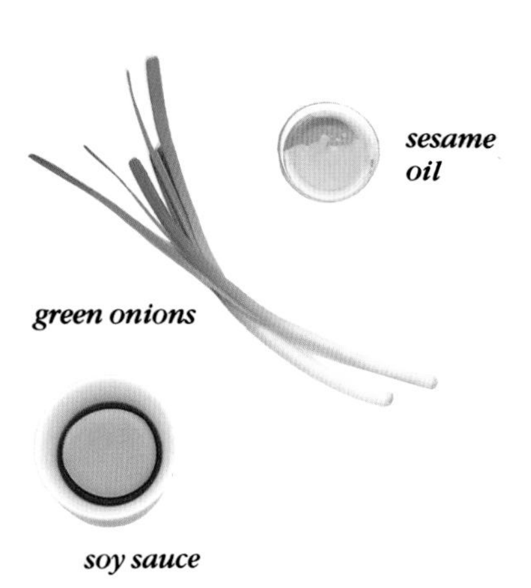

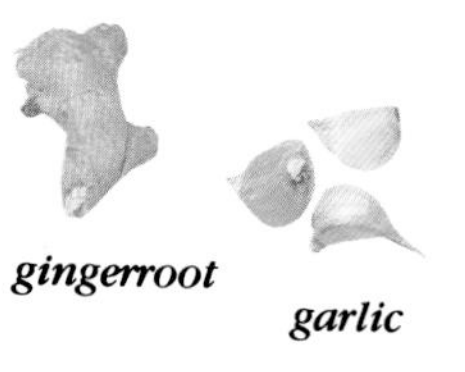

1 Heat the oils in a small saucepan over low heat. Cut the peeled gingerroot into thin slices. Stack the slices and cut into long, thin julienne strips.

2 Turn the strips and cut crosswise into very small dice. Put the diced ginger, garlic, green onions, and chili into the oil and heat for 5 to 7 minutes, to allow the flavors to infuse. Cool and pour into a small bowl and serve with crudités.

VARIATION

Make a sour cream and herb dip by mixing together 1 cup sour cream, 2 finely chopped green onions, and sprigs of fresh herbs such as dill, parsley, and chives. Season with black pepper. You can also add crushed garlic to this dip.

Slicing Fennel

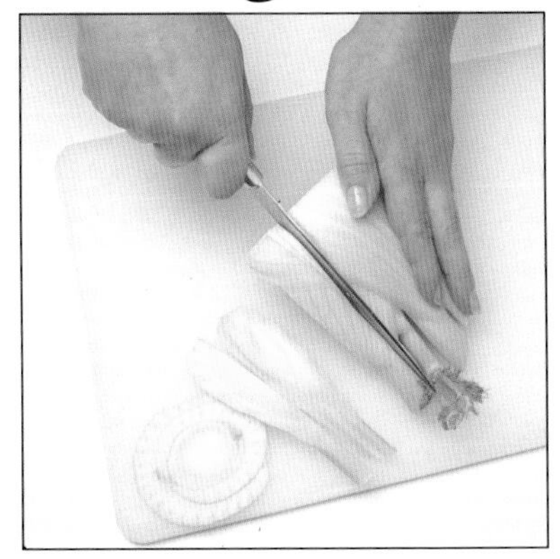

1 Trim the tops and root end of the fennel bulb. If you like, remove the triangular core and cut the bulb in half lengthwise.

2 Cut each half into long strips to serve as crudités.

Tortelloni Kebabs

This hors d'oeuvres is easy to make, and always popular. Any favorite dipping sauce can be substituted, or just drizzle the kebabs with good virgin olive oil and sprinkle with freshly grated Parmesan.

Makes about 64

INGREDIENTS
1 pound fresh cheese-filled tortelloni
2 teaspoons olive oil
basil leaves, to garnish

FOR THE SAUCE
1 × 16-ounce jar roasted red peppers, drained
1 garlic clove, chopped
1 tablespoon olive oil
1 tablespoon balsamic vinegar
1 teaspoon sugar
freshly ground black pepper
2 to 3 dashes hot-pepper sauce

1 Put the ingredients for the sauce into the bowl of a food processor and process until smooth, scraping down the sides once or twice. Strain into a serving bowl and cover until ready to serve.

2 Bring a large saucepan of lightly salted water to a fast boil. Add the tortelloni and cook according to the directions on the package, 8 to 10 minutes. Drain, rinse in warm water and turn into a bowl. Toss with olive oil to prevent sticking. Cover until ready to serve.

3 Use small, 6-inch wooden skewers, and thread a basil leaf and 1 tortelloni onto each skewer. Arrange on a plate and serve warm, or at room temperature with the dipping sauce.

COOK'S TIP

The sauce can be made up to a day in advance or frozen for several weeks.

Hot Corned Beef on a Stick

This quick nibble on a stick is based on the classic New York delicatessen sandwich, pastrami on rye.

Makes 24

INGREDIENTS
vegetable oil for frying
unsliced rye bread with caraway seeds, cut into twenty-four ½-inch cubes
8 ounces corned beef or pastrami, in one piece
mild mustard for spreading
2 pickled cucumbers, cut into small pieces
24 cocktail onions

1 In a heavy-bottomed, medium-size skillet, heat ½ inch of oil. When very hot but not smoking add half the bread cubes and fry for about 1 minute until just golden, turning occasionally. Remove with a slotted spoon and drain on a paper towels. Repeat with the remaining cubes.

2 Cut the corned beef or pastrami into ½-inch cubes and spread one side of each cube with a little mustard.

3 Thread a bread cube onto a skewer, then add a piece of meat with the mustard side against the bread, then a piece of pickled cucumber, and finally an onion. Arrange the skewers on a plate or tray, and serve immediately.

Medjol Dates Stuffed with Cream Cheese

These soft, plump fresh dates make an ideal snack. They are available in most large supermarkets.

Makes 24

INGREDIENTS
24 fresh medjol dates
8 ounces cream cheese, softened
grated peel and juice of ½ orange
1 to 2 tablespoons Amaretto liqueur (optional)
½ cup toasted almonds, coarsely chopped

1 With a small sharp knife, split each date lengthwise and remove the pit. In a small bowl, beat the cream cheese with the orange peel and 2 to 3 tablespoons of the juice. Stir in the Amaretto, if using.

2 Spoon the mixture into a small pastry bag fitted with a medium star or plain tip. Pipe a line of filling into each date, then sprinkle with the nuts.

VARIATION
You can use small dates but they are stickier and more fiddly to prepare.

Hot Crab Dip

This delicious creamy dip with a golden almond crust is served hot, with raw vegetables or crackers.

Makes about 2½ cups

INGREDIENTS
8 ounces cream cheese, at room temperature
2 t– 3 tablespoons milk
1 tablespoon brandy or vermouth
2 green onions, finely chopped
1 to 2 teaspoons Dijon mustard
salt
2 to 3 dashes hot-pepper sauce
1 tablespoon chopped fresh dill or parsley
8 ounces white crabmeat, picked over
3 to 4 tablespoons slivered almonds

1 Preheat the oven to 375°F. In a bowl, using a wooden spoon, beat the cream cheese with all the other ingredients, except the almonds.

2 Spoon the mixture into a small gratin or baking dish and sprinkle with the almonds. Bake for 12 to 15 minutes until the top is golden and the crab mixture hot and bubbling. Serve immediately with a selection of raw vegetables or crackers.

Mini Baked Potatoes with Sour Cream and Chives

Baked potatoes are always delicious, and the toppings can easily be varied—from caviar and smoked salmon to cheese and baked beans.

Makes 36

INGREDIENTS
36 potatoes, about 1½ inches in diameter, well scrubbed
1 cup thick sour cream
3 to 4 tablespoons snipped fresh chives
Kosher salt, for sprinkling

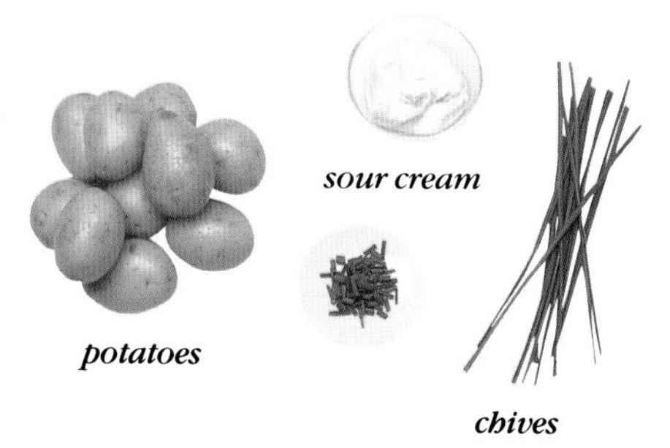

1 Preheat the oven to 350°F. Place potatoes on a baking tray and bake for 30 to 35 minutes, or until tender when pierced with the tip of a knife.

2 To serve, make a cut in the top of each potato and squeeze gently to open. Using the handle of a wooden spoon, make a hole in the center of each potato. Fill each hole with a little sour cream, then sprinkle with the salt and the chives. Serve immediately, or at room temperature.

VARIATION

If your guests are likely to be hungry, use medium-size potatoes. When cooked, cut in half, scoop out the flesh, mash with the other ingredients and spoon the mixture back into the skins. Serve warm.

COOK'S TIP

The potatoes can be baked in advance, then reheated in the microwave on High (100%) for 3 to 4 minutes.

Cheese Balls

These colorful little cheese balls are made in four different flavors, each variety coated with a different herb or seed.

Makes about 48

INGREDIENTS
2 cups cream cheese at room temperature
¼ cup grated sharp Cheddar cheese
½ teaspoon dry mustard powder, prepared
1 teaspoon mango chutney, chopped (optional)
cayenne pepper
salt
2 ounces Roquefort or Stilton cheese
1 tablespoon finely chopped green onions or snipped fresh chives
1 to 2 teaspoons bottled pesto sauce
1 tablespoon chopped pine nuts
1 to 2 garlic cloves, finely chopped
2 tablespoons chopped mixed fresh herbs, such as parsley, tarragon, chives, dill, or cilantro

TO COAT
2 tablespoons paprika
2 tablespoons finely chopped fresh parsley
2 tablespoons toasted sesame seeds
coarsely ground black pepper mixed with poppy seeds

1 Divide the cream cheese equally between 4 small bowls. Into one mix the Cheddar cheese, mustard, and mango chutney, if using. Season with cayenne pepper and a little salt. Into the second bowl, mix the Roquefort or Stilton cheese and green onions or chives and season with a little cayenne.

2 Mix the pesto sauce and pine nuts into the third bowl and season with a little cayenne. Mix the chopped garlic and mixed fresh herbs into the last bowl of cream cheese. Cover and refrigerate all 4 bowls for about 30 minutes until the cheese is firm enough to handle. Roll each of the different cheese mixtures into small balls, keeping them separate.

3 Lightly dust the Cheddar-flavored balls with paprika, rolling to cover completely. Roll the pesto balls in chopped parsley and the Roquefort balls in sesame seeds. Roll the garlic-herb cheese balls in coarsely ground black pepper and poppy seeds. Arrange the balls on leaves, a plate, or in a lined basket and serve with toothpicks.

Crostini with Three Vegetable Toppings

This popular Italian hors d'oeuvre was originally a way of using up leftovers, such as ham, cheese, and pâté.

Makes 24

INGREDIENTS
1 ciabatta or French stick

FOR THE ONION-AND-BLACK-OLIVE TOPPING
1 tablespoon olive oil
2 red onions, thinly sliced
1 teaspoon sugar
½ teaspoon dried thyme
16 kalamata or other oil-cured ripe olives, pitted and halved
bottled tapenade for spreading (optional)
parsley leaves, to garnish

FOR THE PEPPER-AND-ANCHOVY TOPPING
1 × 14 ounce jar Italian roasted red peppers
2 ounces anchovy fillets
extra-virgin olive oil for drizzling
1 to 2 tablespoons balsamic vinegar
1 garlic clove, peeled
2 tablespoons snipped fresh chives, oregano, or sage, to garnish
1 tablespoon capers, to garnish

FOR THE MOZZARELLA-AND-TOMATO TOPPING
pesto sauce for brushing
½ cup thick homemade or bottled tomato sauce or pizza topping
4 ounces good quality mozzarella cheese, cut into 8 thin slices
2 or 3 ripe plum tomatoes, seeded and cut into strips
fresh basil leaves, to garnish

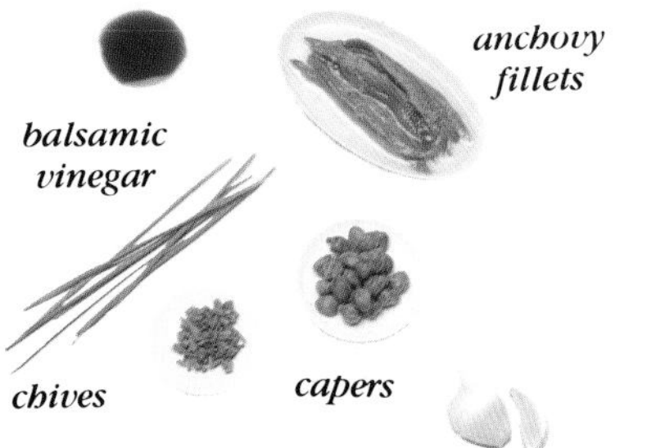

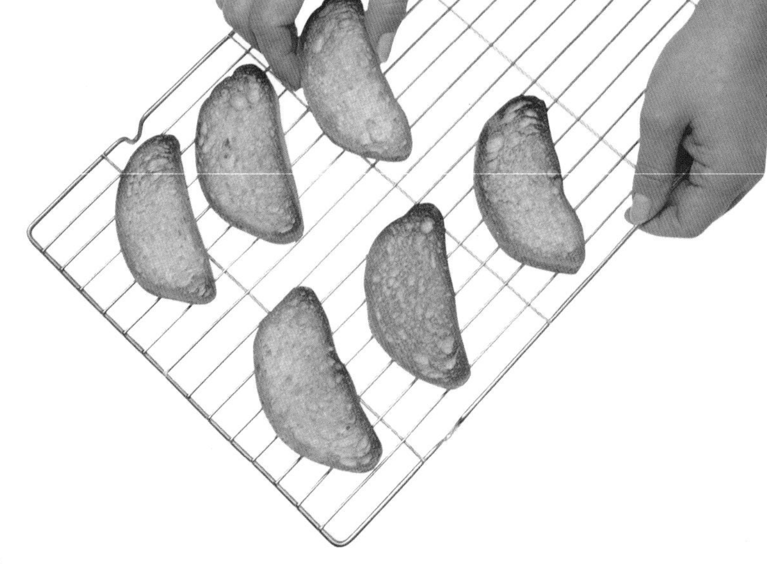

1 Cut the ciabatta or French bread into 24 slices, ½ inch thick. Toast until crisp and golden on both sides. Cool on a wire rack.

2 Prepare the Onion-and-Ripe-Olive Topping. In a heavy-bottomed skillet, heat the olive oil over medium heat and add the onions. Cook slowly for 7 to 10 minutes, stirring frequently, until soft and just beginning to color. Stir in the sugar, thyme, and olives, then remove from the heat to cool. Spread 8 of the toasts with a little tapenade and top with a generous spoonful of the onion mixture. Garnish with parsley.

3 For the Pepper-and-Anchovy Topping, drain the peppers and wipe dry. Cut into ½ inch strips and place in a shallow dish. Rinse and dry the anchovy fillets and add to the peppers. Drizzle with olive oil and sprinkle with the vinegar. Rub 8 toasts with the garlic clove. Arrange the peppers and anchovies on the toasts and sprinkle with herbs and capers. For the Mozzarella-and-Tomato Topping, brush the remaining 8 toasts with pesto sauce and spoon tomato sauce onto each. Arrange a slice of mozzarella cheese on each and cover with the tomato strips. Garnish with basil.

Broiled Brie with Walnuts

This unusual cheese snack looks impressive but requires almost no preparation.

Serves about 16–20

INGREDIENTS
1½ pound wheel of Brie or Camembert cheese
1 tablespoon butter, at room temperature
1 teaspoon Dijon mustard
¼ cup chopped walnuts
French stick, sliced and toasted, to serve

1 Preheat the broiler. In a small bowl, cream together the butter and mustard, and spread evenly over the surface of the cheese. Transfer to a flameproof serving plate, then broil 4 to 6 inches from the heat, for 3 to 4 minutes until the top just begins to bubble.

2 Sprinkle the surface with the walnuts and broil for 2 to 3 minutes longer until the nuts are golden. Serve immediately with the French bread toasts. Allow your guests to help themselves as the whole brie makes an attractive centerpiece.

Spicy Baked Potato Boats

These tasty spiced potato wedges are easy to make, and disappear so quickly it's a good idea to double the recipe!

Makes about 38 wedges

INGREDIENTS
4 medium-size waxy potatoes, scrubbed and unpeeled
1 garlic clove, crushed
1 tablespoon cumin seeds
½ teaspoon ground cilantro
½ teaspoon ground black pepper
⅓ cup virgin olive oil
salt

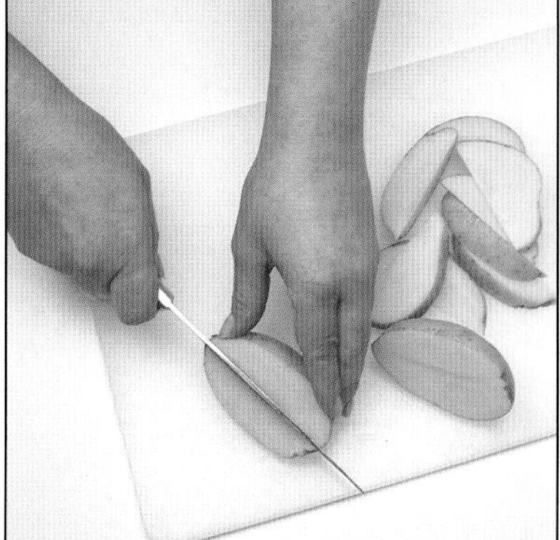

1 Preheat the oven to 400°F. Cut the potatoes into boat-shaped wedges about ¾ inch thick. Place in a large bowl and sprinkle with the cumin garlic, cilantro, black pepper, and olive oil and toss to coat well.

2 Lightly grease a large baking tray (preferably nonstick) and warm in the oven. Arrange the potatoes on baking tray in a single layer. Bake for 30 to 35 minutes until tender and golden brown. Sprinkle with salt and serve hot.

Tiny Cheese Puffs

These bite-sized portions of choux pastry are the ideal accompaniment to a glass of wine.

Makes about 45

INGREDIENTS

1 cup all-purpose flour
½ teaspoon salt
1 teaspoon dry mustard powder
pinch cayenne pepper
1 cup water
½ cup butter, cut into pieces
4 eggs
¾ cup finely diced Gruyère cheese
1 tablespoon chives, finely chopped

1 Preheat the oven to 400°F. Lightly grease 2 large baking trays. Sift together the flour, salt, dry mustard, and cayenne pepper.

2 In a medium-size saucepan, bring the water and butter to a boil over medium-high heat. Remove the pan from the heat and add the flour mixture all at once, beating with a wooden spoon until the dough forms a ball. Return to the heat and beat constantly for 1 to 2 minutes to dry out. Remove from the heat and cool for 3 to 5 minutes.

3 Beat 3 of the eggs in to the dough, one at a time, beating well after each addition. Beat the fourth egg in a small bowl and add a teaspoon at a time beating until the dough is smooth and shiny and falls slowly when dropped from a spoon. (You may not need all the fourth egg; reserve any remaining egg for glazing.) Stir in the diced cheese and chives.

4 Using 2 teaspoons, drop small mounds of dough 2 inches apart on to the baking trays. Beat the reserved egg with 1 tablespoon water and brush the tops with the glaze. Bake for 8 minutes, then reduce the oven temperature to 350°F and bake for 7 to 8 minutes longer until puffed and golden. Remove to a wire rack to cool. Serve warm.

VARIATION

For Ham and Cheese Puffs, add ½ cup finely diced cooked ham with the cheese. For Cheesy Herb Puffs, stir in 2 tablespoons chopped fresh herbs or green onions with the cheese.

COOK'S TIP

The puffs can be prepared ahead and frozen. Reheat in a hot oven for 5 minutes, until crisp, before serving.

Straw Potato Cakes with Caramelized Apple

These little potato cakes resemble *latkes*, a Central European specialty. You must work quickly, because the uncooked potato darkens very rapidly.

Makes about 16

Ingredients

- 1 tablespoon butter
- 1 to 2 eating apples, unpeeled, cored and diced
- 1 teaspoon lemon juice
- 2 teaspoons sugar
- pinch cinnamon
- ¼ cup thick sour cream

For the potato cakes

- oil for frying
- ½ small onion, very finely chopped or grated
- 2 baking potatoes
- salt
- freshly ground black pepper
- flat-leaf parsley, to garnish

1 In a medium-size skillet, melt the butter over medium heat. Add the diced apple and toss to coat. Sprinkle with the lemon juice, sugar, and cinnamon, then cook for 2 to 3 minutes, stirring frequently, until the apples are just tender and beginning to color. Turn into a bowl.

2 Put the grated onion into a bowl. Using a hand or box grater, grate the potatoes onto a clean dish towel and squeeze the potato as dry as possible.

3 Shake into the bowl with the onion and season with the salt and pepper.

4 In a large, heavy-bottomed skillet, heat ½-inch oil, until hot but not smoking. Drop tablespoonfuls of the potato mixture into the oil in batches.

5 Flatten slightly and fry for 5 to 6 minutes. Drain on paper towels. Keep warm. To serve, top each potato cake with 1 teaspoon caramelized apple and then a little sour cream on top. Garnish with flat-leaf parsley.

Cook's Tip

Potato cakes can be prepared in advance and warmed in a preheated 400°F oven for about 5 to 7 minutes, until heated through.

Variation

Omit the caramelized apple and top each cake with a few slices of smoked salmon, sprinkled with snipped chives.

Angels and Devils on Horseback

The combination of bacon with scallops and chicken livers is surprisingly good. Prepare these in advance, then cook them at the last minute.

Makes 24

INGREDIENTS
- 12 bacon slices, rind removed
- 12 scallops, muscle extracted, rinsed and dried
- 12 small chicken livers, gristle and fat removed, dried on paper towels
- salt and freshly ground black pepper
- paprika
- 1 to 2 tablespoons chopped fresh parsley

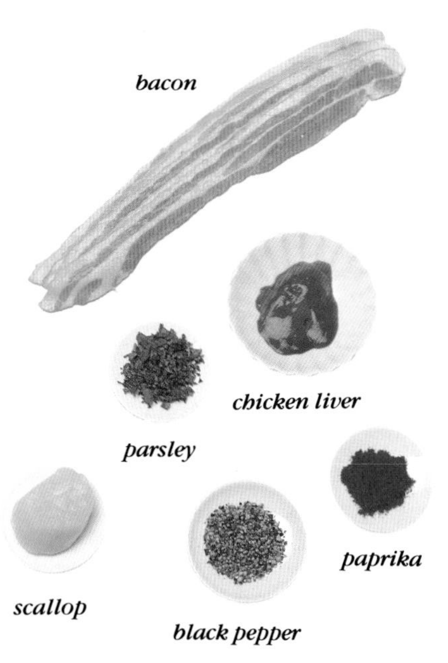

1 Preheat the oven to 450°F. Line a large cookie sheet with foil. Cut the bacon slices in half crosswise and lay them on a counter. Run the back of a large knife blade firmly along each slice to flatten and stretch the bacon.

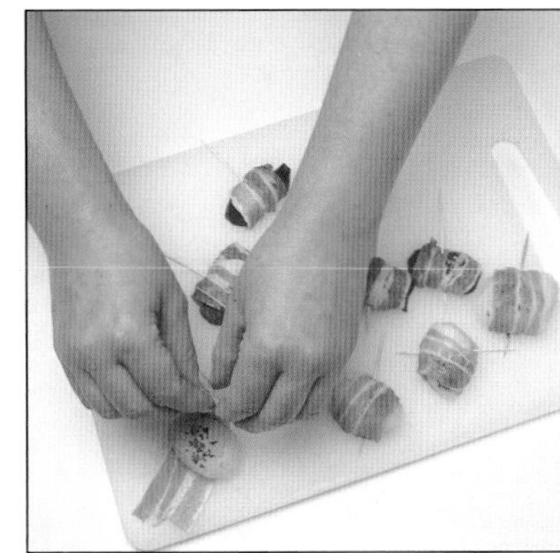

2 Place a scallop on each slice and season with salt, pepper, and paprika. Sprinkle with a little parsley. Place a chicken liver on the remaining rashers and season. Roll the scallops and livers up in the bacon and secure with toothpicks.

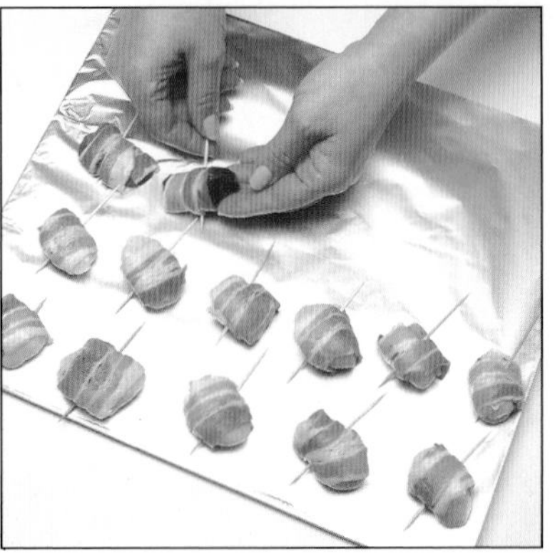

3 Arrange the bacon rolls on the cookie sheet and cook for 8 to 10 minutes until the bacon is crisp and brown and the scallops and livers are just firm to the touch. Serve warm or at room temperature.

VARIATION

Fresh dates stuffed with almonds can be used instead of chicken livers.

Guacamole-filled Cherry Tomatoes

Cherry tomatoes are just the right size for an easy nibble; look for the yellow variety in season. You can make the filling as mild or as spicy as you like.

Makes 24

INGREDIENTS
24 cherry tomatoes
salt
1 large ripe avocado, halved and seed removed
1/3 cup cream cheese
3 to 4 dashes hot-pepper sauce, or to taste
grated peel and juice of 1/2 lime
1 to 2 tablespoons chopped fresh flat-leaf parsley or cilantro

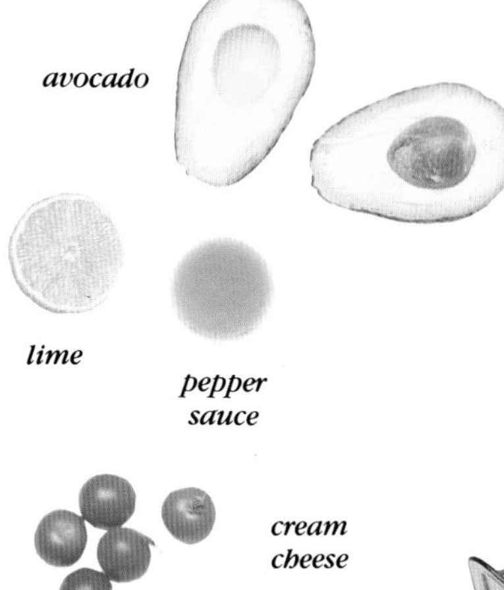

1 Turn the tomatoes on to their sides on a chopping board. With a small sharp knife, cut a slice from the bottom of each tomato. Using the handle of a small spoon, scoop out the seeds and sprinkle the cavities with salt. Turn the tomatoes over and drain on paper towels for at least 30 minutes.

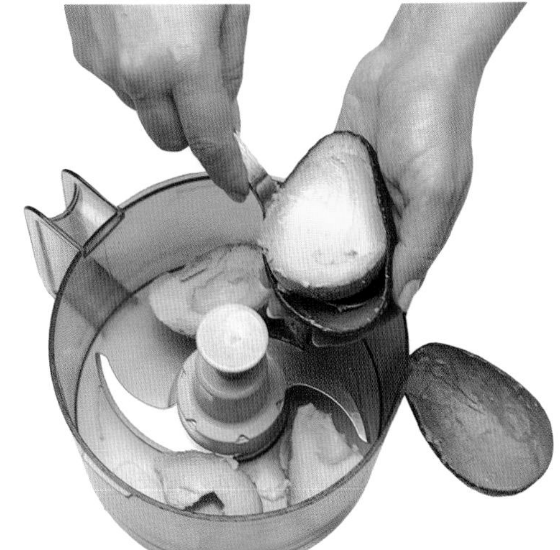

2 Scoop out the flesh of the avocado into the bowl of a food processor and add the cream cheese. Process until very smooth, scraping down the sides of the bowl once or twice. Season with salt, hot-pepper sauce, and the lime peel and juice. Add half the chopped parlsey or cilantro and process to blend.

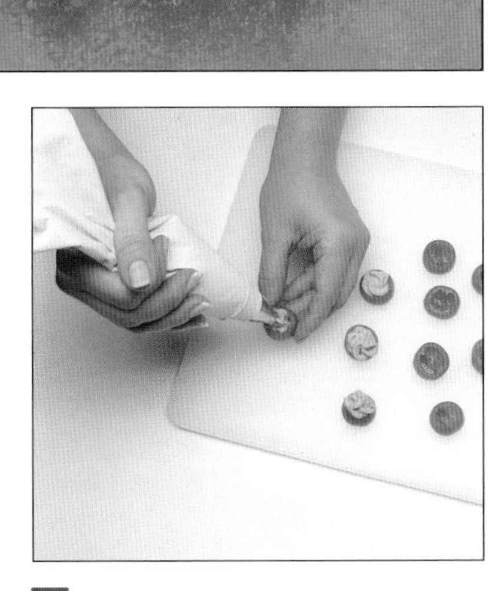

3 Spoon the mixture into a pastry bag fitted with a medium star tip and pipe swirls into the tomatoes. Sprinkle with the remaining parsley or cilantro.

COOK'S TIP

The tomatoes can be prepared the day before and stored, covered, in the refrigerator, ready for filling.

Egg and Bacon on Fried Bread

These miniature "English breakfasts" are an amusing way to serve eggs and bacon as party food.

Makes 12

INGREDIENTS
olive or other vegetable oil for frying
3 or 4 slices white bread
3 slices bacon, diced or sliced
12 quail eggs
cherry tomatoes and flat-leaf parsley, to garnish

1 Preheat the oven to 300°F. Heat about ½-inch oil in a heavy, medium-size skillet. Use a 2-inch round cookie cutter to cut 12 circles from the bread slices.

2 When the oil is hot, but not smoking, add the bread circles and fry for 2 to 3 minutes until golden, turning once. Drain on paper towels. You may need to fry the bread in batches. Arrange the bread circles on a baking tray in a single layer.

3 Pour off all but 1 tablespoon oil and add the bacon pieces. Fry for 3 to 5 minutes until crisp and golden. Drain well on paper towels, then put a few bacon pieces on each fried bread circle.

4 Wipe out the pan and add 2 tablespoons fresh oil to the pan. Break in 4 of the quail eggs and cook for 2 to 3 minutes until set. Carefully remove each egg and set on top of the bacon. Continue cooking the eggs in batches, adding a little more oil if necessary, until all are cooked and arranged on the bread circles.

5 Keep the eggs warm in the preheated oven until ready to serve. Cut the cherry tomatoes into quarters. Just before serving arrange the egg-topped bread on a serving dish and garnish each with a cherry tomato quarter and parsley leaf.

COOK'S TIP

The bread and bacon can be cooked in advance and kept warm or reheated in the oven when ready to serve, but the eggs should not be cooked more than 30 minutes before serving.

VARIATION

If you prefer, instead of frying the eggs, hard-boil them by cooking in boiling water for 2 to 3 minutes. Rinse under cold water and peel. Cut each egg in half and place on the bacon-topped fried bread. Garnish with a piece of chive or a parsley leaf.

Herb-Stuffed Mini Vegetables

These little hors d'oeuvres are ideal for making in advance and assembling and baking at the last minute.

Makes 30

INGREDIENTS
30 mini vegetables, such as zucchini, pattypan squashes, large button mushrooms
fresh basil or parsley, to garnish

FOR THE STUFFING
2 tablespoons olive oil
1 onion, finely chopped
1 garlic clove, finely chopped
1½ cups finely chopped button mushrooms
1 zucchini, finely chopped
1 red pepper, finely chopped
salt and freshly ground black pepper
⅓ cup orzo pasta or long-grain rice
⅓ cup Italian passata (puréed and strained tomatoes)
½ teaspoon dried thyme
½ cup chicken stock
1 to 2 teaspoon chopped fresh basil or parsley
½ cup shredded mozzarella or fontina cheese

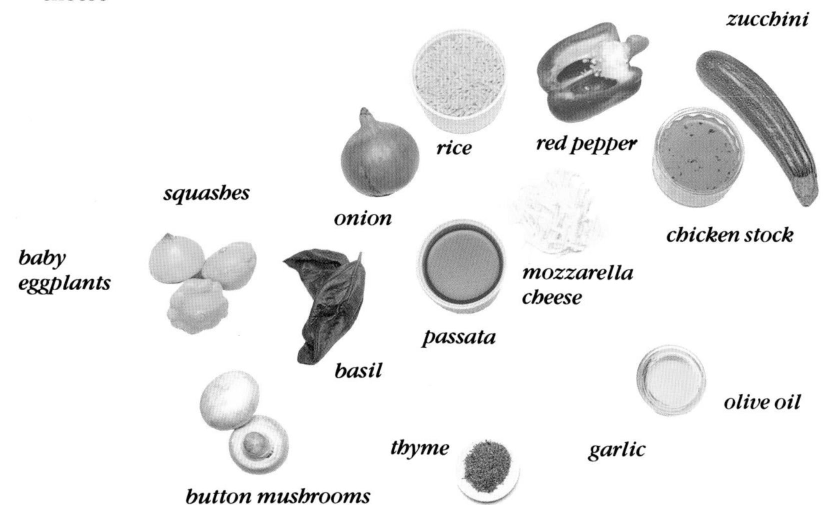

1 Prepare the stuffing. In a medium-size skillet or heavy-bottomed saucepan, heat the oil over medium heat. Add the onion and cook for 2 to 3 minutes until just tender. Stir in the garlic, mushrooms, zucchini, and red pepper. Season with salt and pepper and cook for 2 to 3 minutes until the vegetables begin to soften.

2 Stir in the pasta or rice and the passata, then add the thyme and stock and bring to a boil, stirring frequently. Reduce the heat and simmer for 10 to 12 minutes until all the liquid has evaporated and the mixture is thickened. Remove from the heat and cool slightly. Stir in the basil or parsley and cheese and set aside.

4 Remove the stems from the center of the mushrooms. If you like, the mushrooms can be blanched like the zucchini or tossed with oil and baked in the oven for 10 minutes at 350°F. Allow to cool before stuffing.

VARIATION

If you wish, after the first 10 minutes of baking remove from the oven, sprinkle the vegetables with grated parmesan, and broil for 3 minutes.

3 Prepare the vegetables. Drop the zucchini and pattypan squashes into a large pot of boiling water and cook for 3 minutes. Drain and refresh under cold running water. Trim a thin slice from the length of the zucchini and the bottom of the squashes so they sit firmly on a plate. Trim ¼-inch off the tops and scoop out the centers with a small spoon or melon baller; try not to make any holes in the bottom.

5 Preheat the oven to 350°F. Using a teaspoon carefully fill the prepared vegetables with stuffing. Arrange the vegetables in 2 large baking dishes. Pour in enough boiling water just to cover the bottoms and prevent the vegetables sticking.

6 Cover the dishes tightly with foil and bake for 10 minutes. Uncover and bake for about 5 minutes longer until the fillings are hot and bubbling. Remove from the dish to a wire rack or paper-towel-lined cookie sheet if any water remains. Cool slightly, garnish with basil or parsley and serve warm or at room temperature.

Corn Muffins with Ham

These delicious little muffins are simple to make. If you like, serve them unfilled with a pot of herb butter.

Makes 24

INGREDIENTS
scant ½ cup yellow cornmeal
⅔ cup all-purpose flour
2 tablespoons sugar
1½ teaspoons baking powder
½ teaspoon salt
4 tablespoons butter, melted
½ cup whipping cream
1 egg, beaten
1 or 2 jalapeño or other medium-hot chilies, seeded and finely chopped (optional)
pinch cayenne pepper
butter for spreading
grainy mustard or mustard with honey for spreading
2 ounces oak-smoked ham

1 Preheat the oven to 400°F and lightly grease a mini muffin pan with twenty-four 1½-inch cups. In a large bowl, combine the cornmeal, flour, sugar, baking powder, and salt. In another bowl, whisk together the melted butter, cream, beaten egg, chopped chilies, if using, and the cayenne pepper.

2 Make a well in the cornmeal mixture, pour in the egg mixture and gently stir into the dry ingredients just enough to blend (do not overbeat—the batter does not have to be smooth).

3 Drop 1 tablespoon batter into each muffin cup, then bake for 12 to 15 minutes, until golden and just firm to the touch. Remove the pan to a wire rack to cool slightly, then turn out the muffins onto the rack and leave to cool completely.

4 With a sharp knife, split the muffins and spread each bottom half with a little butter and mustard. Cut out small circles of ham with a round cookie cutter, or cut the ham into small squares, and place it on the buttered muffins. Sandwich together each muffin and serve.

COOK'S TIP

Muffins can be made in advance and stored in airtight containers. Bring to room temperature or warm slightly before filling and serving.

Feta, Pimiento and Pine Nut

Delight your guests with these tempting pizzas. Substitute goat cheese for the feta if you prefer.

Makes 24

INGREDIENTS
2 quantities Basic or Superquick Pizza Dough
4 tbsp olive oil
2 tbsp black olive tapenade
6 oz feta
1 large canned pimiento, drained
2 tbsp chopped fresh thyme
2 tbsp pine nuts
black pepper
thyme sprigs, to garnish

pimiento

thyme

feta cheese

tapenade

pine nuts

1 Preheat the oven to 425°F. Divide the dough into 24 pieces and roll out each one on a lightly floured surface to a small oval, about ⅛ in thick. Place the ovals, well apart, on greased baking sheets and prick all over with a fork. Brush each one with 2 tbsp of the oil.

2 Spread a thin layer of the black olive tapenade on each oval and crumble the feta over.

3 Cut the pimiento into thin strips and pile on top.

4 Sprinkle each one with thyme and pine nuts. Drizzle the remaining oil over and grind over plenty of black pepper. Bake for 10–15 minutes until crisp and golden. Garnish with thyme sprigs and serve immediately.

Smoked Salmon Pizzettes

Mini pizzas topped with smoked salmon, crème fraîche and lumpfish caviar make an extra special party canapé.

Makes 10–12

INGREDIENTS
1 packet pizza dough mix
1 tablespoon snipped fresh chives
1 tablespoon olive oil
3–4 ounces smoked salmon, cut into strips
4 tablespoons crème fraîche
2 tablespoons black lumpfish caviar
chives, to garnish

1 Preheat the oven to 400°F. Prepare the dough as directed on the packet. Mix in the chives.

2 Roll out the dough on a lightly floured surface to about ⅛ in thick. Using a 3 in plain round cutter stamp out 10–12 circles.

3 Place the bases well apart on two greased baking sheets, prick all over with a fork, then brush with the oil. Bake for 10–15 minutes until crisp and golden.

4 Arrange the smoked salmon on top, then spoon on the crème fraîche. Spoon a tiny amount of lumpfish caviar in the center and garnish with chives. Serve immediately.

Buffalo-Style Chicken Wings

This fiery-hot fried chicken recipe is said to have originated in the town of Buffalo, New York, but is now popular everywhere. Serve it with traditional Blue-cheese Dip and celery sticks.

Makes 48

INGREDIENTS
24 plump chicken wings, tips removed
vegetable oil for frying
salt
6 tablespoons butter
¼ cup hot-pepper sauce, or to taste
1 tablespoon white or cider vinegar
celery sticks, to serve

FOR THE BLUE-CHEESE DIP
4 ounces blue cheese, such as Danish blue
½ cup mayonnaise
½ cup sour cream
2 to 3 green onions, finely chopped
1 garlic clove, finely chopped
1 tablespoon white or cider vinegar

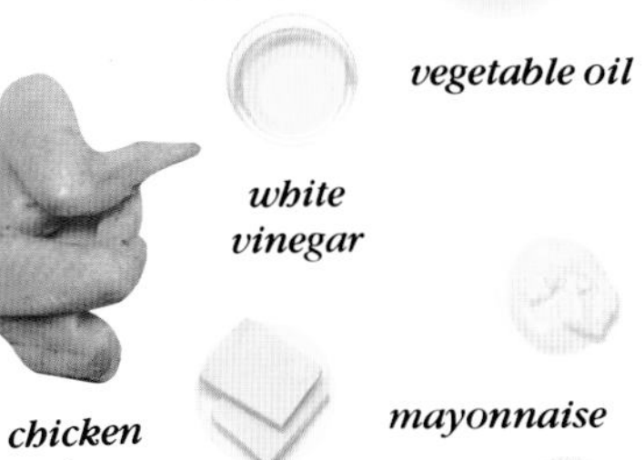

1 To make the dip, use a fork to gently mash the blue cheese against the side of a bowl. Add the mayonnaise, sour cream, green onions, garlic, and vinegar and stir together until well blended. Refrigerate until ready to serve.

2 Using kitchen scissors or a sharp knife, cut each wing in half at the joint to make 48 pieces in all.

3 In a large saucepan or wok, heat 2 inches of oil until hot but not smoking. Fry the chicken wing pieces in small batches for 8 to 10 minutes until crisp and golden, turning once. Drain on paper towels. Season and arrange in a bowl.

4 In a small saucepan over medium-low heat, melt the butter. Stir in the hot-pepper sauce and vinegar and immediately pour over the chicken, tossing to combine. Serve hot with the blue-cheese dip and celery sticks.

Spicy Sun-Dried Tomato Pizza Wedges

These spicy pizza wedges can be made with or without the pepperoni or sausage.

Makes 32

INGREDIENTS
3 to 4 tablespoons olive oil
2 onions, thinly sliced
2 garlic cloves, chopped
8 ounces sliced mushrooms
8 ounces can chopped tomatoes
8 ounces pepperoni or cooked Italian-style spicy sausage, chopped
4 ounces drained and sliced sun-dried tomatoes, packed in oil
1 teaspoon chili flakes
1 teaspoon dried oregano
1 pound bottled marinated artichoke hearts, well drained and cut into quarters
8 ounces shredded mozzarella cheese
4 tablespoons freshly grated Parmesan cheese
fresh basil leaves, to garnish
pitted ripe olives, to garnish

FOR THE DOUGH
1 package pizza-dough mix
cornmeal, for dusting
virgin olive oil for brushing and drizzling

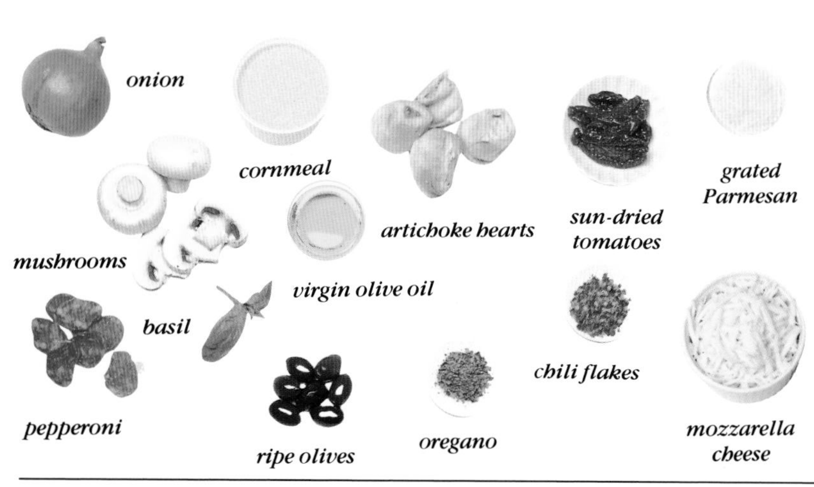

1 Prepare the pizza dough according to the package directions, set aside to rise.

2 Prepare the sauce. In a large, deep skillet, heat the oil over medium-high heat. Add the onions and cook for 3 to 5 minutes until softened. Add the garlic and mushrooms and cook for 3 to 4 minutes more until the mushrooms begin to color.

3 Stir in the chopped tomatoes, pepperoni or sausage, chili flakes, and oregano and simmer for 20 to 30 minutes, stirring frequently, until the sauce is thickened and reduced. Stir in the sun-dried tomatoes, and then set aside to cool slightly.

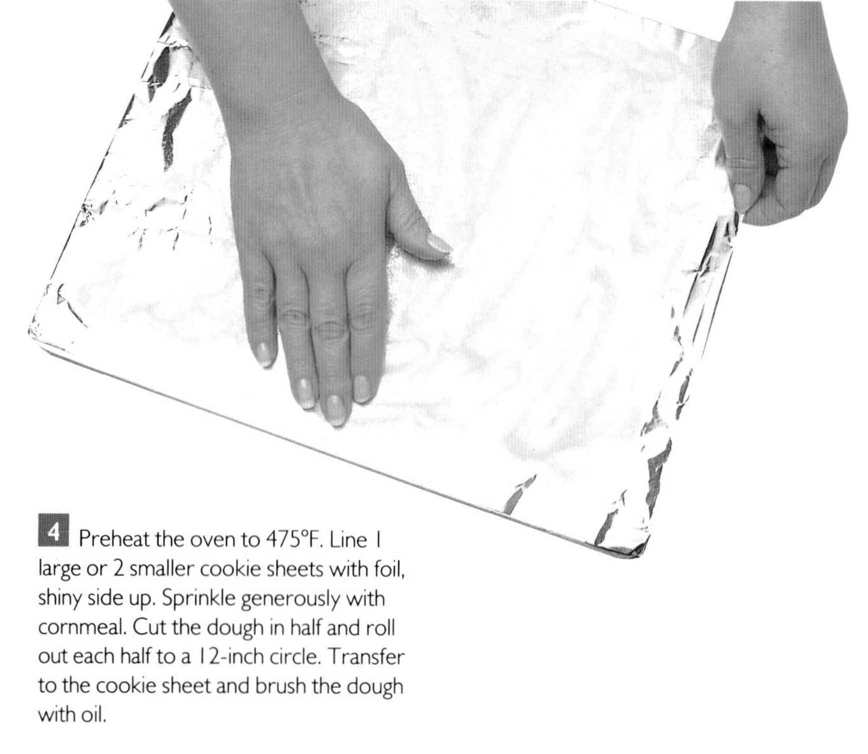

4 Preheat the oven to 475°F. Line 1 large or 2 smaller cookie sheets with foil, shiny side up. Sprinkle generously with cornmeal. Cut the dough in half and roll out each half to a 12-inch circle. Transfer to the cookie sheet and brush the dough with oil.

5 Divide the spicy tomato sauce between the dough circles, spreading to within ½-inch of the edge. Bake for 5 minutes on the lowest shelf of the oven. Arrange half the artichoke hearts over each, sprinkle evenly with the mozzarella and a little Parmesan. Bake each one in the oven on the bottom shelf for 12 to 15 minutes longer, until the edge of the crust is crisp and brown and the topping is golden and bubbling. Remove to a wire rack to cool slightly.

6 Slide the pizzas onto a cutting board and cut each into 16 thin wedges. Garnish each wedge with a ripe olive and basil leaf and serve immediately.

Tortilla Squares

The Spanish tortilla is like the Italian frittata—a flat, baked omelet. Plain or filled, it is always popular.

Makes about 60 squares

INGREDIENTS

4 to 6 tablespoons olive oil, plus extra for brushing
1 large onion, thinly sliced
2⅓ cups thinly sliced baking potatoes
2 garlic cloves, finely chopped
½ teaspoon dried thyme
salt and freshly ground black pepper
8 eggs
1 to 2 teaspoons dried oregano or basil
¼ teaspoon cayenne pepper or hot-pepper sauce, to taste
1 cup frozen peas, thawed and drained
2 to 3 tablespoons freshly grated Parmesan cheese
red pepper, to garnish

onion *potatoes* *peas* *olive oil* *garlic clove* *Parmesan cheese* *egg* *cayenne pepper* *black pepper* *oregano* *thyme*

1 In a large, deep, and preferably nonstick, skillet, heat 4 tablespoons of the oil over medium heat. Add the onions and potatoes and cook for 8 to 10 minutes, stirring frequently, until just tender. Add the garlic, thyme, salt, and pepper and cook for 2 minutes longer. Remove from the heat and cool slightly.

2 Preheat the oven to 300°F. Lightly brush an 8- × 12-inch square or 10-inch round baking dish with 2 tablespoons oil. In a mixing bowl, beat the eggs with the oregano or basil, salt, and cayenne pepper until well mixed. Stir in the peas.

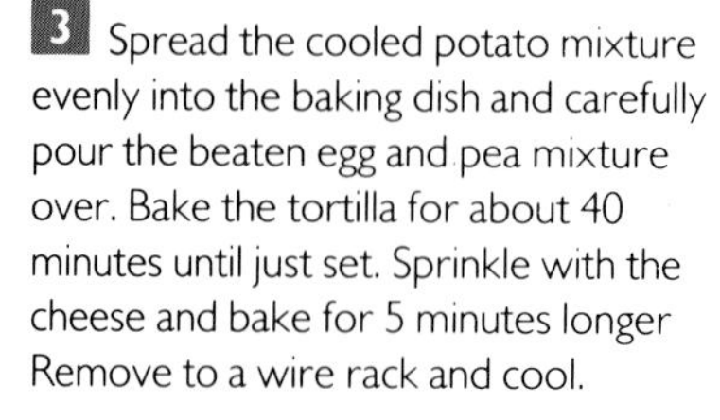

3 Spread the cooled potato mixture evenly into the baking dish and carefully pour the beaten egg and pea mixture over. Bake the tortilla for about 40 minutes until just set. Sprinkle with the cheese and bake for 5 minutes longer Remove to a wire rack and cool.

4 Carefully unmold the tortilla, cut into 60 small squares. Serve warm or at room temperature with toothpicks, and garnished with pieces of red pepper.

COOK'S TIP

If you like, serve a small bowl of chili sauce as a dip for the tortilla squares.

Monti Cristo Triangles

These opulent little sandwiches are stuffed with ham, cheese, and turkey, dipped in egg, and fried in butter and oil. They are rich and very filling.

Makes 64

INGREDIENTS
16 slices firm-textured, thin-sliced white bread
½ cup butter, softened
8 slices oak-smoked ham
3 to 4 tablespoons grainy mustard
8 slices Gruyère or Swiss cheese
3 to 4 tablespoons mayonnaise
8 slices turkey or chicken breast
4 or 5 eggs
¼ cup milk
salt and white pepper
1 teaspoon Dijon mustard
vegetable oil for frying
butter for frying
pimiento-stuffed green olives, to garnish
flat-leaf parsley leaves, to garnish

1 Arrange 8 of the bread slices on the work surface and spread with half the softened butter. Lay 1 slice of ham on each slice of bread and spread with a little grainy mustard. Cover with a slice of cheese and spread with a little mayonnaise, then cover with a slice of turkey or chicken breast. Butter the remaining bread slices and use to complete the sandwiches. Cut off the crusts, trimming to an even square.

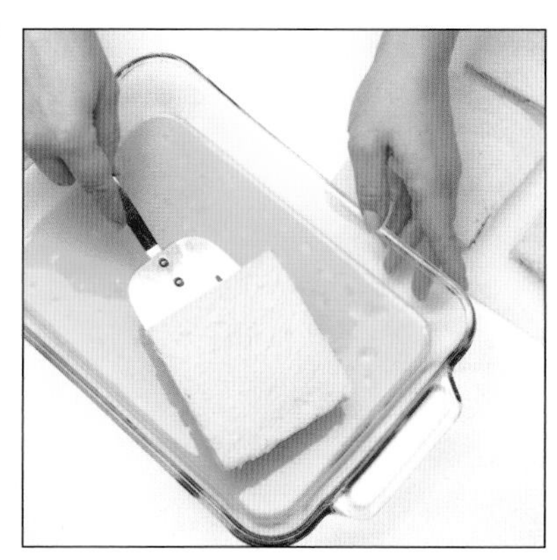

2 In a large, shallow baking dish, beat the eggs, milk, salt and pepper, and Dijon mustard until well combined. Soak the sandwiches in the egg mixture on both sides until the egg has been absorbed.

3 Heat about ½-inch of oil and melted butter in a large, heavy skillet until hot but not smoking. Gently fry the sandwiches in batches for 4 to 5 minutes until crisp and golden, turning them once. Add more oil and butter as necessary. Drain on paper towels.

4 Transfer the sandwiches to a cutting board and cut each into 4 triangles, then cut each in half again to make 64 triangles. Thread a parsley leaf and olive onto a toothpick, then stick into each triangle and serve immediately.

COOK'S TIP

These sandwiches can be prepared ahead and reheated in a preheated oven at 400°F for 6 to 8 minutes.

French Country Terrine

This versatile terrine can be served in slices, used to fill sandwiches, or cut into small cubes and threaded onto toothpicks with tiny gherkins or onions.

Makes 1 terrine or loaf

COOK'S TIP

The pork can be ground in a hand grinder if you do not have a food processor. Alternatively, ask your butcher or the assistant at the supermarket meat counter to coarsely grind a piece of pork leg or shoulder.

INGREDIENTS
- 1 pound leeks, trimmed, cut in half lengthwise and washed
- 1 tablespoon butter
- 2 or 3 garlic cloves, finely chopped
- 2¼ pounds lean pork, well trimmed, cut into pieces
- 5 ounces smoked bacon
- 1½ teaspoons chopped fresh thyme or 1 teaspoon dried thyme
- ½ teaspoon dried sage
- ¼ teaspoon grated nutmeg
- ½ teaspoon quatre épices or ground allspice
- ½ teaspoon salt
- 1 teaspoon freshly ground black pepper
- 2 bay leaves
- cherry tomatoes, to garnish

TO SERVE
- French country bread or a French stick, sliced and toasted
- French grainy mustard
- pickled gherkins
- Belgian endive leaves

1 Thinly slice the leeks. In a large, heavy-bottomed saucepan, melt the butter and stir in the leeks. Cook over low heat, covered, for 10 minutes, stirring occasionally. Stir in the garlic and cook for 5 to 7 minutes longer, until the leeks are tender. Remove from the heat to cool.

2 Put the pork pieces in the bowl of a food processor (you may need to work in 2 or 3 batches) and process carefully until coarsely chopped; do not overprocess. Transfer to a large bowl.

3 Reserve 2 or 3 slices of bacon and process the remaining slices. Add to the pork mixture with the leeks, thyme, sage, quatre épices, nutmeg, and salt and pepper. Using a wooden spoon or your hands, mix until well combined.

4 Preheat the oven to 350°F. Grease a heavy, nonstick 6¼-cup terrine or bread pan. Drape the reserved bacon slices diagonally across the pan, pressing into the corners. Put the bay leaves down the center of the pan bottom, then spoon in the terrine mixture, pressing it into the sides and corners. Smooth the top of the terrine and then cover with foil.

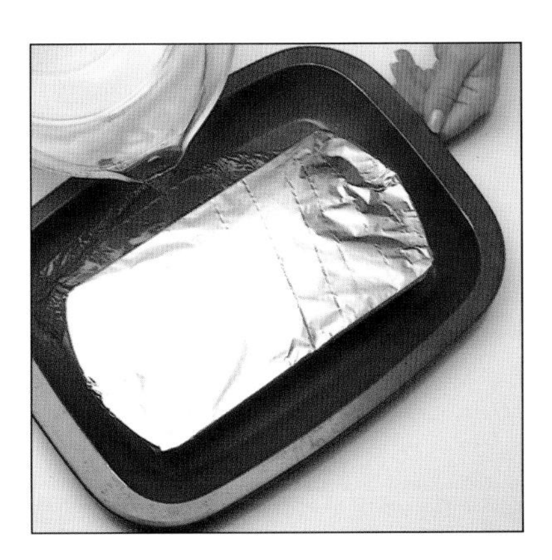

5 Put the terrine in a roasting pan and pour in enough boiling water to come half way up the sides of the terrine. Bake for 1¼ hours. Cool completely. Place a foil-covered piece of board, cut to fit, on top of the terrine. Weigh it down with 2 heavy cans or weights and refrigerate overnight.

6 To serve, loosen the edges of the terrine with a knife and turn out onto a serving dish or cutting board. Scrape off any congealed fat or juices and cut into thin slices. Serve on endive leaves or pieces of toasted French bread, spread with French grainy mustard and garnished with gherkins and cherry tomatoes.

Scandinavian Open-Faced Sandwiches

The Swedes and Danes are famous for their open-faced sandwiches, which are often served as part of a *smörgåsbord*—a huge party buffet of hot and cold dishes.

Makes 16 halves

INGREDIENTS

ROAST BEEF WITH HORSERADISH CREAM

3 to 4 tablespoons mayonnaise
1 tablespoon horseradish sauce
2 to 3 dashes hot-pepper sauce
4 slices rye bread
4 slices very rare tender roast beef
diced sweet-and-sour pickled cucumber
watercress, to garnish

GRAVLAX WITH HONEY-DILL MUSTARD SAUCE

2 to 3 tablespoons mayonnaise
2 teaspoons Dijon mustard
1 tablespoon honey
1 teaspoon vegetable oil
1 tablespoon chopped fresh dill
4 slices whole-wheat bread
4 to 8 slices gravlax (cured salmon), depending on slice size
cucumber slices, to garnish

SMOKED CHICKEN AND AVOCADO WITH LIME

8 ounces smoked chicken breast half, skin removed
1 small ripe avocado, diced
¼ cup garlic mayonnaise
juice of ½ lime
4 slices pumpernickle or black rye bread
1 to 2 teaspoons butter, softened
curly endive leaves, optional
lime slices, to garnish

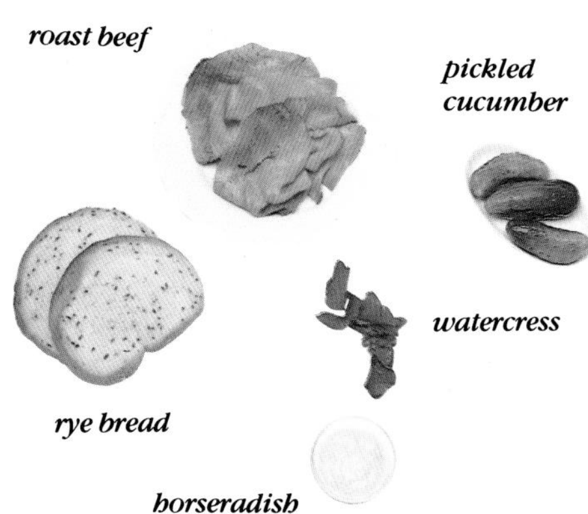

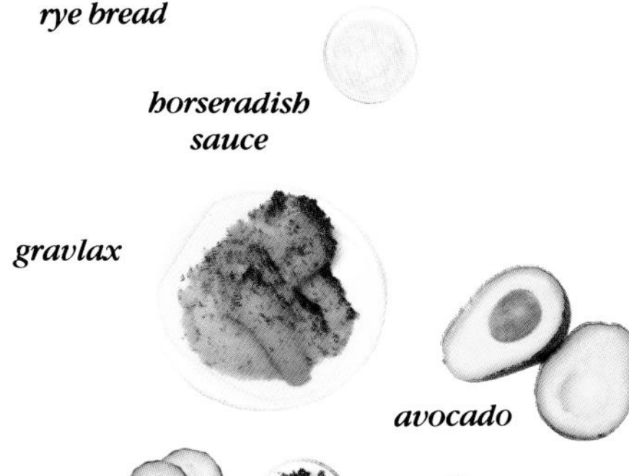

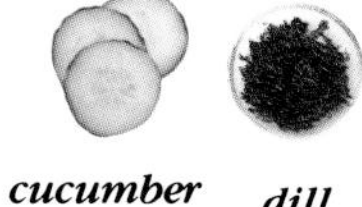

COOK'S TIP

All sandwiches are best made immediately before serving. The toppings can be prepared in advance, and then assembled at the last minute.

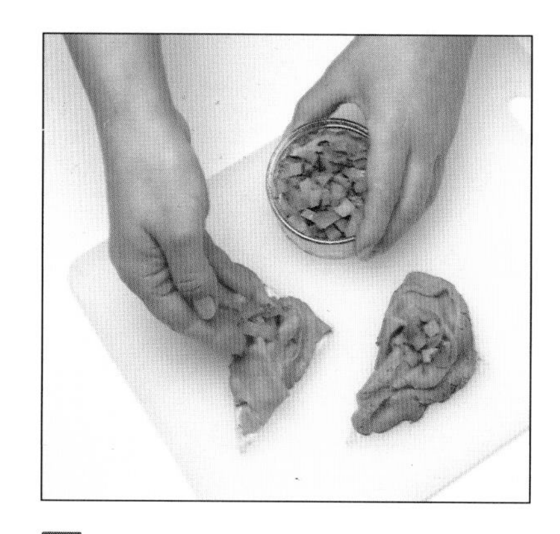

1 To make the Roast Beef with Horseradish, in a small bowl, combine the mayonnaise and horseradish and hot-pepper sauces according to taste. Spread the rye bread slices with the horseradish sauce. Arrange the roast beef in folds for a more attractive appearance on the bread and cut each slice into 2 triangles. Sprinkle each with a little pickled cucumber chopped into cubes and garnish with watercress.

2 For the Gravlax with Honey Dill Mustard, in a small bowl,combine the mayonnaise, mustard, honey, oil, and dill. Reserve 1 to 2 tablespoons for the garnish. Cut each slice of bread into 2 triangles and spread with the horseradish sauce. Arrange the gravlax on each triangle overlapping slightly, and garnish with cucumber slices and the remaining sauce.

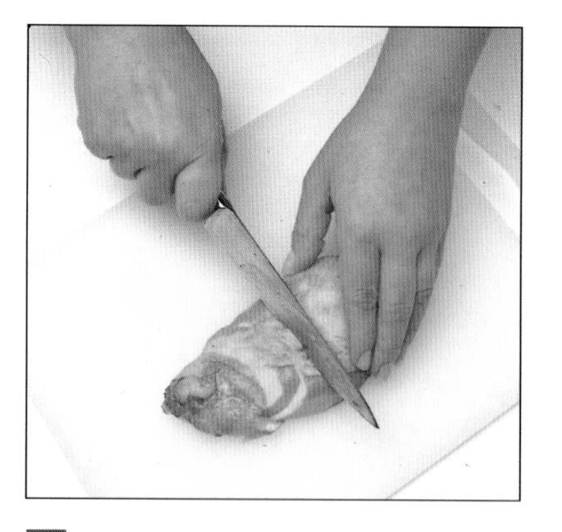

3 For the Smoked Chicken and Avocado, slice the chicken. Toss the diced avocado in a bowl with the mayonnaise and lime juice until just blended.

4 Spread the pumpernickle bread slices with a little softened butter and cut each slice into 2 triangles. Arrange a few slices of chicken on the bread and top with a spoonful of the avocado mixture. Garnish with lime slices and a sprig of mint.

Greek Meze with Pita Crisps

Meze are a selection of Greek hors d'oeuvres, and these three dips are quick and easy to make in a food processor. They also go well together—serve them with raw vegetables or these wonderful pita crisps.

INGREDIENTS

FOR THE TZATZIKI (Makes about 3 cups)
- 2½ cups plain yogurt
- 1 large cucumber
- 1 teaspoon salt
- 1 or 2 garlic cloves, finely chopped
- 2 or 3 tablespoons chopped fresh mint or 1 tablespoon dried mint
- 1 or 2 tablespoons virgin olive oil (optional)
- mint sprigs, to garnish

FOR THE HUMMUS (Makes about 2½ cups)
- heaped 2 cups canned garbanzo beans
- 3½ tablespoons tahini (sesame paste)
- 3½ tablespoons freshly squeezed lemon juice
- 1 to 2 garlic cloves, crushed
- salt
- cayenne pepper, to taste
- 1 or 2 tablespoons olive oil
- 1 or 2 tablespoons chopped fresh parsley or cilantro
- olive or sesame oil for drizzling

FOR THE SMOKY EGGPLANT DIP (Makes about 2 cups)
- 1 large eggplant (about 1 pound)
- 4 tablespoons freshly squeezed lemon juice
- 4 tablespoons tahini or mayonnaise
- 2 or 3 garlic cloves, chopped
- salt
- 2 tablespoons virgin olive oil
- 2 tablespoons chopped fresh parsley

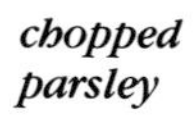

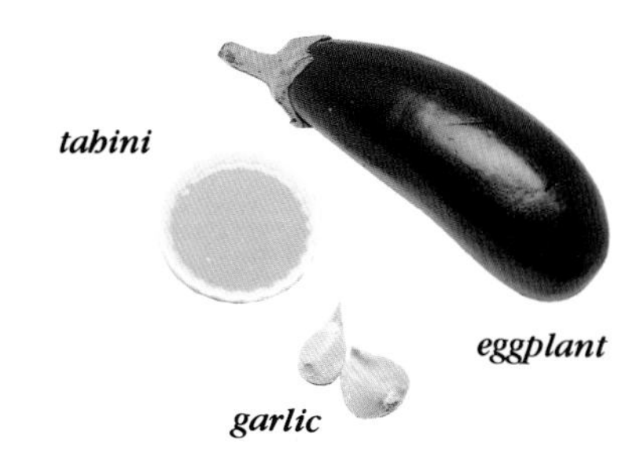

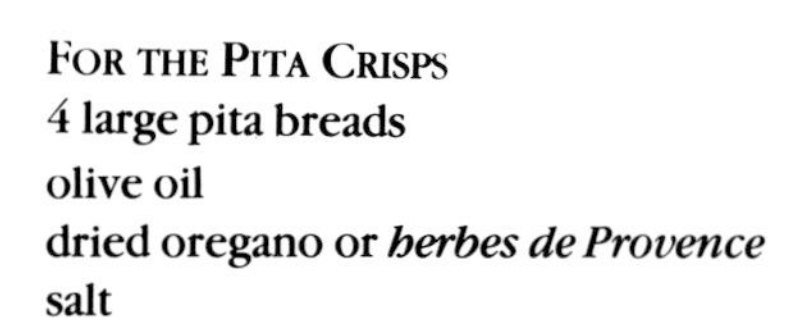

FOR THE PITA CRISPS
- 4 large pita breads
- olive oil
- dried oregano or *herbes de Provence*
- salt

1 To make the Tzatziki, peel the cucumber and cut it lengthwise into quarters. Cut out the seeds, chop finely, and place in a colander. Sprinkle with the salt and leave to drain for about 1 hour. Pat dry with paper towels. Put the yogurt in a bowl and stir in the drained cucumber, garlic, and mint. Slowly blend in the olive oil, if using. Spoon into a serving bowl, garnish with mint and refrigerate.

2 To make the Hummus, drain the garbanzo beans, reserving the liquid, set aside a few beans for garnishing. Put the remaining beans in a food processor and add the tahini, lemon juice, and garlic. Process until very smooth, scraping down the side of the bowl occasionally. Season with the salt and cayenne pepper and process to blend.

3 With the machine running, slowly pour in 1 to 2 tablespoons olive oil and some of the reserved bean liquid to thin the purée if necessary. Pour into a shallow serving bowl and spread it up the side of the bowl, swirling with the back of a spoon. Pour a little extra olive oil or sesame oil in the center, add the reserved garbanzos, and sprinkle with cayenne pepper. Sprinkle with the chopped parsley or cilantro.

4 To make the Smoky Eggplant Dip, if possible, barbecue the eggplant over a charcoal fire for about 30 minutes. Alternatively, place on a rack with a tray placed below, in the center of a preheated oven, 400°F. Bake for about 30 minutes or until soft, turning, frequently. Remove from the oven. When cool enough to handle, scoop out the flesh into the bowl of a food processor. Add the lemon juice, tahini or mayonnaise, garlic, salt to taste, olive oil, and 1 tablespoons of the parsley. Process for 1 to 2 minutes until very smooth, scraping the sides of the bowl once or twice. Pour into a shallow bowl and garnish with the remaining parsley.

5 To make the Pita Crisps, preheat the oven to 350°. Split the pitas in half lengthwise to form 2 thin layers. Brush generously with olive oil and sprinkle with a little dried oregano or *herbes de Provence* and a pinch of salt. Cut each in half lengthwise, then into triangles and place on 2 large cookie sheets. Bake the pita triangles for 15 to 20 minutes until golden and crisp. Cool on the cookie sheets, then store in an airtight container until ready to serve.

COOK'S TIP

You can, of course, serve these dips with warmed pita bread, but for parties these crisps are ideal because they don't spoil, and they are cooked in advance, so do make the extra effort—it's worth it!

Corn Fritters with Red-Pepper Salsa

The salsa can also be served with grilled chicken or vegetable kebabs. Add the chilies slowly and according to your taste, as they can be very hot.

Makes about 48

INGREDIENTS
corn or other vegetable oil
1 pound frozen or canned corn kernals, drained
1 cup all-purpose flour
½ cup yellow cornmeal
1 cup milk
2 teaspoons baking powder
2 teaspoons sugar
1 teaspoon salt
½ teaspoon nutmeg
½ teaspoon cayenne pepper
4 eggs, lightly beaten
cilantro leaves, to garnish

FOR THE SALSA
4 ounces cherry tomatoes, chopped
½ cup frozen or canned corn kernels, drained
1 red-pepper, cored and finely chopped
½ small red onion, finely chopped
juice of 1 lemon
2 tablespoons olive oil
2 tablespoons chopped fresh cilantro
1 to 2 fresh chilies, seeded and finely chopped
salt
½ teaspoon sugar

1 Prepare the salsa at least 2 hours ahead. Combine the ingredients in a bowl, crushing them lightly with the back of a spoon to release the juices. Cover and refrigerate until ready to use.

2 In a bowl, combine 2 tablespoons of the oil with the corn, flour, cornmeal, milk, baking powder, sugar, salt, nutmeg, cayenne pepper, and eggs until just blended; do not overbeat. If the batter is too stiff, stir in a little more milk or water.

3 In a large, heavy-based skillet, heat ½-inch oil until hot but not smoking. Drop tablespoonsful of the batter into the hot oil and cook for 3 to 4 minutes until golden, turning each fritter over once. Drain on paper towels. Arrange on cookie sheets and keep warm for up to 1 hour in an oven at 325°F.

4 Arrange the corn fritters on a serving plate. Top each with a spoonful of salsa and garnish with a cilantro leaf. Serve hot or warm.

COOK'S TIP

The salsa can be made up to a day in advance. Keep in the refrigerator, covered.

Mini Sausage Rolls

These miniature versions of old-fashioned sausage rolls are always popular—the Parmesan cheese gives them an extra-special flavor.

Makes about 48

INGREDIENTS
1 tablespoon butter
1 onion, finely chopped
12 ounces good-quality sausagemeat
1 tablespoon dried mixed herbs, such as oregano, thyme, sage, tarragon, or dill
salt and pepper
¼ cup finely chopped pistachio nuts (optional)
12 ounces puff pastry dough
4 to 6 tablespoons freshly grated Parmesan cheese
1 egg, lightly beaten, for glazing
poppy seeds, sesame seeds, fennel seeds, or aniseeds for sprinkling

VARIATION

Phyllo pastry can be used instead of puff dough for a very light effect. Depending on the size of the phyllo sheets, cut into 8 pieces 10 × 3 inches. Brush 4 of the sheets with a little melted butter or vegetable oil and place a second phyllo sheet on top. Place one sausage log on each of the layered sheets and roll up and bake as below.

1 In a small skillet, over medium heat, melt the butter. Add the onion and cook for about 5 minutes until softened. Remove from the heat and cool. Put the onion, sausagemeat, herbs, salt and pepper, and nuts (if using) in a mixing bowl and stir together until blended.

2 Divide the sausage mixture into 4 equal portions, then roll into thin sausages about 10 inches long; set aside.

3 On a lightly floured surface, roll out the dough to about ⅛ inch thick. Cut the pastry into 4 strips 10 × 3 inches long. Place a long sausage on each dough strip and sprinkle each with a little Parmesan cheese.

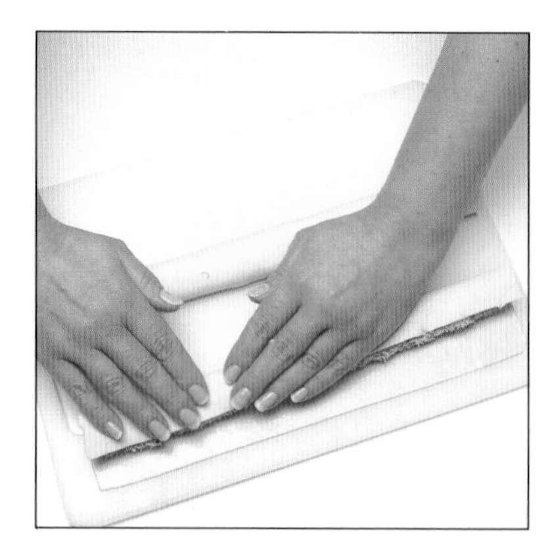

4 Brush one long edge of each of the dough strips with the egg glaze and roll up to enclose each long sausage. Set them seam-side down and press gently to seal. Brush each with the egg glaze and sprinkle with one type of seeds. Repeat with remaining dough strips and different seeds.

5 Preheat the oven to 425°F. Lightly grease a large cookie sheet. Cut each of the dough rolls into 1 inch pieces and arrange on the cookie sheet. Bake for 15 minutes until the pastry is crisp and brown. Serve warm or at room temperature.

Smoked Trout Mousse in Cucumber Cups

This delicious creamy mousse can be made in advance and kept for 2 or 3 days in the refrigerator. Serve it in crunchy cucumber cups, or simply with crudités.

Makes about 24

INGREDIENTS
½ cup cream cheese, softened
2 green onions, chopped
1 to 2 tablespoons chopped fresh dill or parsley
1 teaspoon horseradish sauce
8 ounces smoked trout fillets, flaked and any fine bones removed
2 to 4 tablespoons heavy cream
salt
cayenne pepper, to taste
2 cucumbers
dill sprigs, to garnish

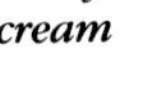

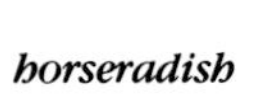

VARIATION

For Smoked Salmon Mousse, use smoked salmon pieces instead of smoked trout.

1 Put the cream cheese, green onions, dill, and horseradish sauce into the bowl of a food processor and process until well blended. Add the trout and process until smooth, scraping down the side of the bowl once. With the machine running, pour in the cream until a soft mousselike mixture forms. Season, turn into a bowl, and refrigerate for at least 15 minutes.

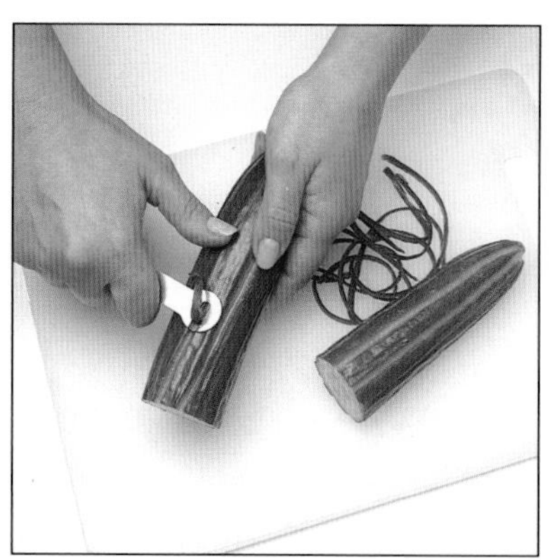

2 Using a canelle knife or vegetable peeler, score the length of each cucumber to create a striped effect. Cut each cucumber into ¾-inch-thick slices. Using a small spoon or melon baller, scoop out the seeds from the center of each round.

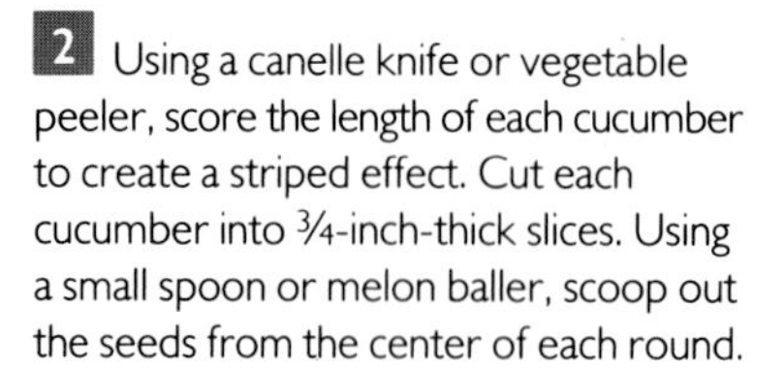

3 Spoon the mousse into a pastry bag fitted with a medium star tip and pipe swirls of the mixture into the cucumber slices. Refrigerate until ready to serve. Garnish each with a small sprig of dill.

Carpaccio Rolls with Anchovy Mayonnaise

This classic hors d'oeuvre of raw beef makes an extravagant but delicious treat.

Makes about 24

INGREDIENTS
8 ounces beef tenderloin, cut from the narrow end and frozen for 1 hour
4 tablespoons virgin olive oil
1 tablespoon lemon juice
freshly ground black pepper
arugula or flat-leaf parsley, to garnish
capers, to garnish
Belgian endive leaves or short celery sticks, to serve

FOR THE ANCHOVY MAYONNAISE
4 to 6 anchovy fillets, drained
1 cup homemade or good quality mayonnaise
1 tablespoon capers, rinsed, drained and chopped
1 small garlic clove, crushed
2 tablespoons freshly grated Parmesan cheese

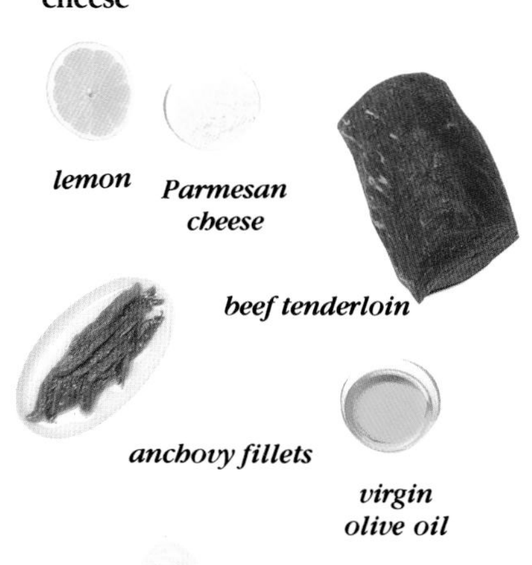

1 To make the Anchovy Mayonnaise, in a bowl, mash the anchovy fillets with a fork, then beat in the mayonnaise, capers, garlic, and Parmesan cheese until well blended.

2 Slice the beef into as many wafer-thin pieces as possible and arrange flat on a cookie sheet. Brush each piece with the olive oil and sprinkle with a little lemon juice and black pepper.

3 Place about ½ a teaspoon Anchovy Mayonnaise in the center of each beef slice, then fold the beef into quarters, or roll it up.

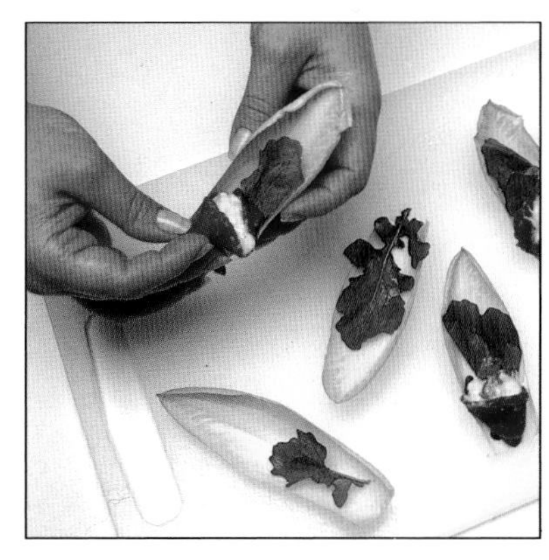

4 To serve, place a rocket leaf at the bottom of an endive leaf and place a rolled or folded up slice of beef on top. Sprinkle with a few capers if you like. If you prefer, skewer each beef parcel with a toothpick and serve on its own.

Spicy Crab Cakes

These are miniature versions of a classic New England specialty. Use fresh crabmeat if your budget allows.

Makes about 30

INGREDIENTS
8 ounces crabmeat, drained and picked over
1½ cups fresh white bread crumbs
2 green onions, finely chopped
1 to 2 tablespoons chopped fresh dill or parsley
1 egg, lightly beaten
¼ cup mayonnaise
1 tablespoon Dijon mustard
1 to 2 tablespoons lemon juice
salt
1 small green chili, seeded and chopped (optional)
2 to 3 dashes hot-pepper sauce
fine dried bread crumbs for coating
vegetable oil for frying

FOR THE SEAFOOD COCKTAIL SAUCE
½ cup horseradish sauce
1 to 2 tablespoons mayonnaise
¼ cup tomato ketchup
lemon juice, to taste

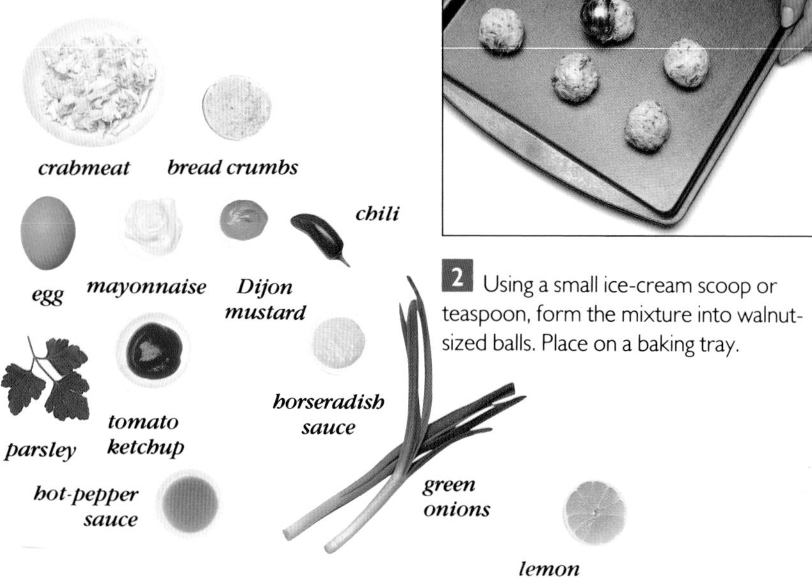

1 To make the Seafood Cocktail Sauce, combine all the ingredients. Refrigerate. For the crab cakes, in a large bowl, combine all the ingredients, except the oil and dried breadcrumbs.

2 Using a small ice-cream scoop or teaspoon, form the mixture into walnut-sized balls. Place on a baking tray.

3 Put the dried bread crumbs in a shallow plate and coat the crab balls, a few at a time, rolling to cover completely. Place on a baking tray and flatten each ball slightly until ½ inch thick. Refrigerate for at least 30 minutes.

4 In a large, heavy-bottomed skillet heat ½-inch oil until hot but not smoking. Fry the crab cakes, in batches, for about 2 minutes until crisp and golden, turning once. Serve hot or warm with the sauce.

Smoked Salmon Nests on Wild-Rice Pancakes

The nutty flavor of wild rice provides a perfect foil to the smoky richness of the salmon, in this elegant hors d'oeuvre.

Makes about 24

INGREDIENTS
8 ounces smoked salmon
3 to 4 tablespoons creamed horseradish sauce
fresh chives or dill, to garnish

FOR THE WILD-RICE PANCAKES
½ cup all-purpose flour
salt and white pepper
1 egg, lightly beaten
¼ cup milk
1⅓ cups cooked wild-rice
2 tablespoons chopped chives or dill
vegetable oil for frying

1 To make the Wild-Rice Pancakes, sift the flour, and salt and pepper into a medium-size bowl and make a well in the center. Put the egg and milk in the well and, using a wire whisk or electric beater on slow speed, gradually bring in the flour from the edges to form a smooth batter. Stir in the wild rice and chives or dill.

2 In a large, heavy-bottomed skillet, heat 2 to 3 tablespoons oil over medium-high heat until very hot. Drop tablespoonsful of the batter into the pan and flatten slightly. Fry for 2 to 3 minutes until golden, turning once. Drain on paper towels and keep warm.

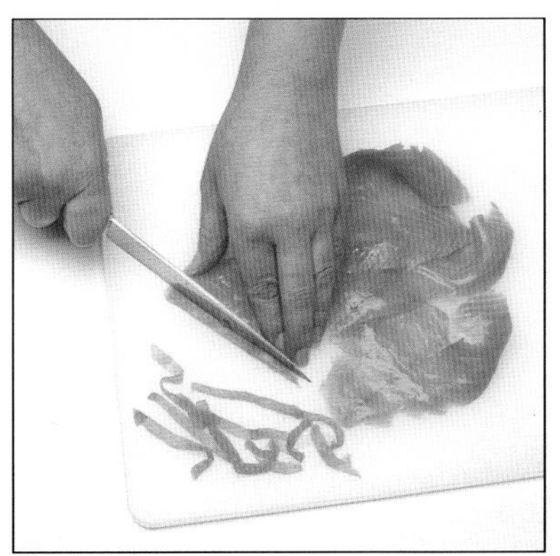

3 With a sharp knife, cut the smoked salmon into thin strips. Spoon a little horseradish cream onto each pancake and top with a pile of salmon strips, twisting to form a nest. If you like, garnish with extra dollops of horseradish cream and fresh chives or dill.

VARIATION

The same effect can be achieved more simply by making little bread slices, instead of pancakes. Cut out 2-inch circles from white or whole-wheat sliced bread and toast lightly under a broiler on both sides before adding the topping.

Foie Gras Pâté in Phyllo Cups

This is an extravagantly rich hors d'oeuvre—save it for a special occasion.

Makes about 24

INGREDIENTS
- 8 ounces canned foie gras pâté or other fine liver pâté, at room temperature
- 4 tablespoons butter, softened
- 2 to 3 tablespoons Cognac or other brandy (optional)
- 3 to 6 sheets fresh or defrosted phyllo pastry
- 3 tablespoons butter, melted
- chopped pistachio nuts, to garnish

phyllo pastry

foie gras pâté

pistachio nuts

butter

Cognac

COOK'S TIP

The pâté and pastry are best eaten soon after preparation. If preparing ahead and refrigerating, be sure to bring back to room temperature before serving.

1 Preheat the oven to 400°F. Grease a muffin pan with twenty-four 1½-inch cups. Stack the phyllo sheets on a work surface and cut into 2½-inch squares. Cover with a damp towel.

2 Keeping the rest of the phyllo squares covered, place one square on the counter and brush lightly with melted butter, then turn and brush the other side. Butter a second square and place it over the first at an angle. Butter a third square and place at an angle over the first 2 sheets to form an uneven edge.

3 Press the layers into the cup of the bun tray. Continue with the remaining pastry and butter until all the cups are filled.

4 Bake the phyllo cups for 4 to 6 minutes until crisp and golden, then remove and cool in the pan for 5 minutes. Carefully remove each phyllo cup to a wire rack and cool completely.

5 In a small bowl, beat the pâté with the softened butter until smooth and well blended. Add the Cognac or brandy to taste, if using. Spoon into a pastry bag fitted with a medium star tip and pipe a swirl into each cup. Sprinkle with pistachio nuts. Refrigerate until ready to serve.

Grilled Asparagus Tips with Easy Hollandaise Sauce

Delicate asparagus tips and buttery rich Hollandaise Sauce make a classic combination and a delicious treat.

Makes 24

INGREDIENTS
24 large asparagus spears
oil for brushing
freshly grated Parmesan cheese for sprinkling

FOR THE HOLLANDAISE SAUCE
¾ cup butter, cut into pieces
2 egg yolks
1 tablespoon lemon juice
1 tablespoon water
salt and cayenne pepper

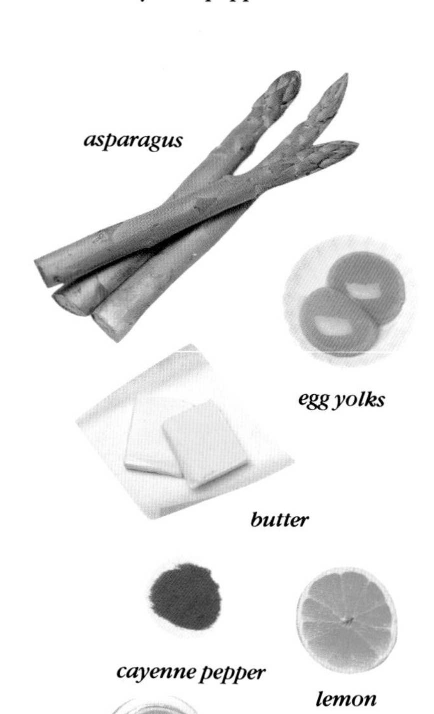

1 To make the Hollandaise Sauce, melt the butter in a small saucepan and skim off any foam which bubbles to the top.

2 Put the egg yolks, lemon juice, and water into a blender or a food processor. Season with salt and cayenne pepper and blend or process to mix. With the machine running, slowly pour in the hot butter in a thin stream; do not pour in the milky solids on the bottom of the pan.

3 Using a vegetable peeler, peel the asparagus spears. Cut off the stalks to leave tips of about 5 inches.

4 Cook the tips in boiling salted water for 2 to 3 minutes until just tender; do not overcook. Refresh under cold water to stop them cooking, then cover until ready to serve.

5 Preheat the broiler. Line a cookie sheet with foil and brush each asparagus tip with a little oil. Sprinkle each tip with a little Parmesan cheese, then broil for 2 to 3 minutes, turning once. Arrange the asparagus on a plate, and serve with the Hollandaise Sauce for dipping.

COOK'S TIP

Keep the Hollandaise Sauce warm by storing it in a vacuum flask until ready to store.

VARIATION

Wrap each asparagus tip in a thin strip of bacon or prosciutto and brush with oil before broiling. If you like, cut the remainder of the asparagus spears into 3-inch pieces and broil them, for slightly longer, as well.

Marinated Mussels

This is an ideal recipe to prepare and arrange well in advance. Remove from the refrigerator 15 minutes before serving to allow the flavors to develop.

Makes 48

Ingredients
- 2¼ pounds fresh mussels, large if possible
- ¾ cup dry white wine
- 1 garlic clove, well crushed
- freshly ground black pepper
- ½ cup olive oil
- ¼ cup lemon juice
- 1 teaspoon hot chili flakes
- ½ teaspoon apple pie spice
- 1 tablespoon Dijon mustard
- 2 teaspoons sugar
- 1 teaspoon salt
- 1 to 2 tablespoons chopped fresh dill or cilantro
- 1 tablespoon capers, diced, drained and chopped if large

1 With a stiff kitchen brush, under running cold water, scrub the mussels to remove any sand and barnacles; pull out and remove any beards. Discard any open shells that will not shut when tapped.

Cook's Tip

Mussels can be prepared ahead and marinated for up to 24 hours. To serve, arrange the mussel shells on a bed of crushed ice, well-washed seaweed, or even kosher salt to stop them wobbling on the plate.

2 In a large flameproof casserole or saucepan over high heat, bring the white wine to a boil with the garlic and freshly ground black pepper. Add the mussels and cover. Reduce the heat to medium and simmer for 2 to 4 minutes until the shells open, stirring occasionally.

3 Meanwhile, in a large bowl, combine the olive oil, lemon juice, chili flakes, apple pie spice, Dijon mustard, sugar, salt, chopped dill or cilantro, and capers.

4 Discard any mussels with closed shells. With a small sharp knife, carefully remove remaining mussels from their shells, reserving 48 shells for serving. Add the mussels to the marinade. Toss the mussels to coat well, then cover and refrigerate for 6 to 8 hours, or overnight, stirring gently from time to time.

5 With a teaspoon, place one mussel with a little marinade in each shell. Arrange on a platter and cover until ready to serve.

A Trio of Tartlets

Tender pastry topped with luscious ingredients always look irresistible—and taste even better! Vary the toppings according to the occasion.

Makes about 24

INGREDIENTS
1 1/3 cups all-purpose flour
1/2 tsp salt
6 tablespoons butter, cut into pieces
1 egg yolk beaten with 2 to 3 tablespoons cold water

FOR THE SCRAMBLED EGG AND CAVIAR
1 tablespoon butter
2 eggs, lightly beaten
salt and white pepper
1 tablespoon heavy cream or crème fraîche
1 to 2 tablespoons caviar or lumpfish caviar (optional)

FOR THE SMOKED SALMON AND LEEK
1/2 cup heavy cream
1 leek, split lengthwise, washed and thinly sliced
salt and freshly ground black pepper
pinch of grated nutmeg
4 ounces smoked salmon, sliced very thinly
dill sprigs, to garnish

FOR THE ASPARAGUS AND BRIE
1 tablespoon butter
6 asparagus stalks cut into 1 1/2-inch pieces
salt
2 ounces Brie, rind removed and sliced

flour

salt

eggs

caviar

heavy cream

butter

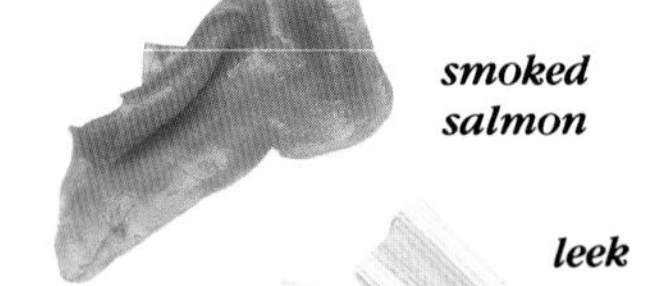
smoked salmon

leek

nutmeg

Brie

asparagus

1 To make the dough, put the flour, salt, and butter into the bowl of a food processor and process quickly, until the mixture resembles fine crumbs. Reserve 1 tablespoon of the egg mixture. With the processor running, pour in the remaining egg mixture until the dough just begins to come together (do not allow it to form a ball or it may toughen). If the dough is too dry, add a little more water and process briefly again. Put the dough onto a piece of plastic wrap and use the plastic to push it together and flatten to form a disk shape. Wrap tightly; refrigerate for 1 1/2 hours.

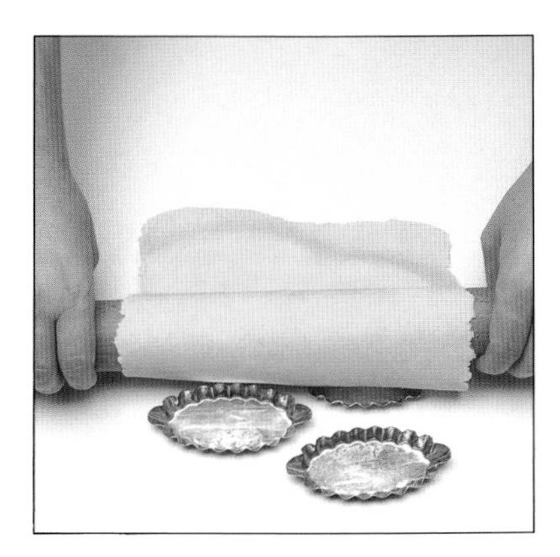

2 On a lightly floured counter, roll out the dough until 1/8 inch thick. Lay out about twelve 2-inch tartlet pans. Lay the dough over the pans and press out. Reroll the trimmings and repeat. Line 24 cases, then prick the bottoms with a fork and refrigerate for 30 minutes.

3 Preheat the oven to 375°F. Put a small piece of crumbled foil into each shell and place on a baking tray. Bake for 6 to 8 minutes until the edges are golden. Remove the foil and brush each pastry bottom with a little of the reserved egg mixture. Bake for 2 minutes until dry. Transfer to a wire rack to cool.

4 Prepare the fillings: for the Scrambled Egg and Caviar, melt the butter in a small skillet over medium-low heat. Season the eggs with salt and white pepper and add to the pan. Cook the eggs slowly, stirring constantly, until smooth and just set. Remove from the heat and stir in the cream or crème fraîche. Spoon into 8 of the pastry shells. Just before serving, garnish each tartlet with a pinch of caviar. Serve warm or at room temperature.

5 For the Smoked Salmon and Leek filling, bring the cream to a simmer in a pan over medium heat. Add the leeks and cook, stirring frequently, until just tender and the cream is completely reduced. Season with salt, pepper, and a pinch of nutmeg. Spoon into 8 of the pastry shells and top with smoked salmon strips and sprigs of dill just before serving. Serve warm or at room temperature.

6 For the Asparagus and Brie filling, melt the butter in a skillet over medium-high heat. Add the asparagus pieces and stir-fry for 2 to 3 minutes until tender. Divide among the remaining tartlet shells and sprinkle each with a little salt. Divide the Brie among the tartlets. Just before serving, return to the oven for 1 to 2 minutes until the Brie softens. Serve straight away before the cheese hardens.

COOK'S TIP

If you do not have 24 tartlet pans, you will need to work in batches. Divide the dough in half or quarters and refrigerate the portion you are not using immediately.

Hazelnut Sablés with Goat Cheese and Strawberries

Sablés are little French cookies, made from egg yolk and butter. Crisp and slightly sweet, they contrast perfectly with the tangy goat cheese and juicy strawberries.

Makes about 24

INGREDIENTS
- 6 tablespoons butter, at room temperature
- 1 cup all-purpose flour
- 6 tablespoons blanched hazelnuts, lightly toasted and ground
- 2 tablespoons superfine sugar
- 2 egg yolks beaten with 2 to 3 tablespoons water
- 4 ounces goat cheese
- 4 to 6 large strawberries, cut into small pieces
- chopped hazelnuts, to decorate

VARIATION

These sablés are ideal served with fruit. Beat 6 tablespoons cream cheese with 1 tablespoon confectioners' sugar and a little lemon or orange peel. Spread a little on the sablé and top with a few pieces of sliced kiwi fruit, peach, nectarine and a few raspberries or cut-up strawberries.

1 To make the dough, put the butter, flour, ground hazelnuts, sugar, and beaten egg yolks into the bowl of a food processor and process until a smooth dough forms.

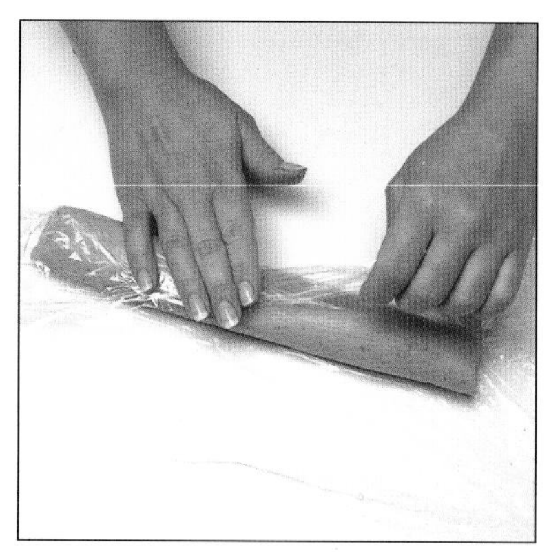

2 Scrape the dough out onto a sheet of plastic wrap and use the plastic to shape the dough into a log about 1½ inches in diameter. Wrap tightly and refrigerate for 2 hours, or overnight, until very firm.

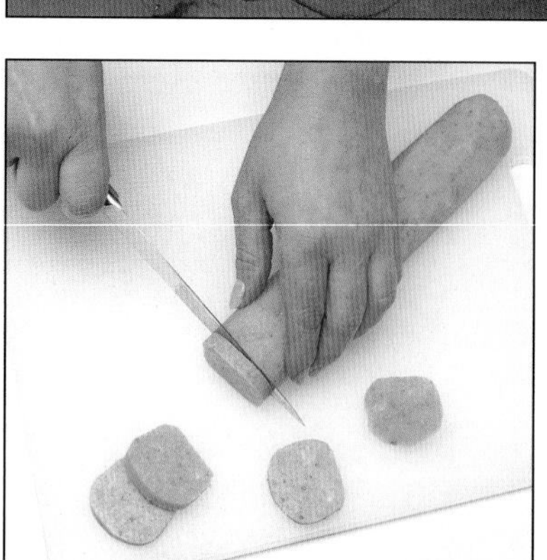

3 Preheat the oven to 400°F and line a large cookie sheet with nonstick parchment paper. With a sharp knife, slice the dough into ¼-inch thick slices and arrange on the cookie sheet. Bake for 7 to 10 minutes until golden brown. Remove to a wire rack to cool and crisp slightly.

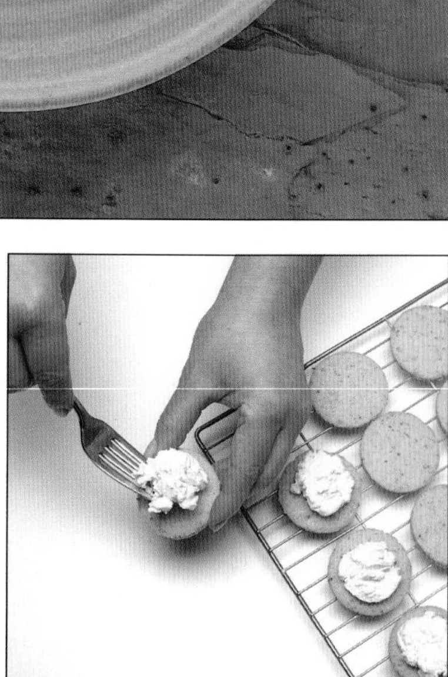

4 On a plate, crumble the goat cheese into small pieces. Mound a little goat cheese on to each sablé, top with a piece of strawberry and sprinkle with a few hazelnuts. Serve warm.

Rich Chocolate and Fruit Fondue

This sumptuous fruit fondue, with its rich, delicious sauce, makes a lavish finish to a party.

Makes $1\frac{1}{2}$ cups

INGREDIENTS
a selection of mixed fruit, such as kumquats, apple, peach and pear slices, banana slices, clementine segments, seedless grapes, cherries, peeled lychees, mango and papaya cubes, cut figs and plums
lemon juice

FOR THE CHOCOLATE FONDUE
8 ounces good-quality semisweet chocolate, chopped
2 tablespoons corn syrup
2 tablespoons whipping cream
2 to 3 tablespoons brandy or orange-flavored liqueur

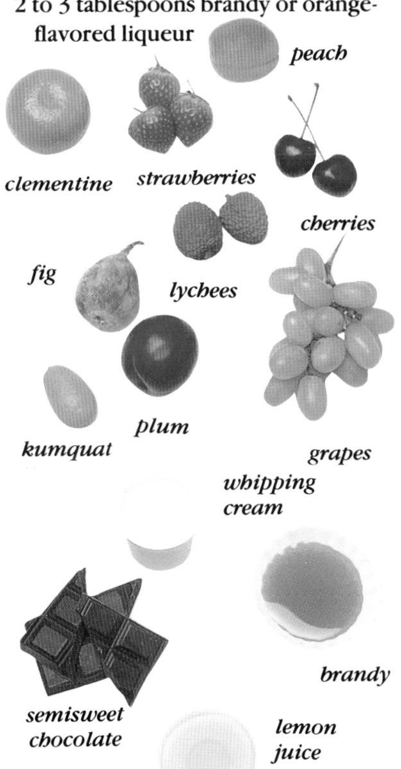

1 Arrange the fruits in an attractive pattern on a large serving dish. Brush any cut-up fruit such as apples, pears, or banana with lemon juice to prevent darkening. Cover and refrigerate until ready to serve.

2 In a medium-size saucepan over medium-low heat, combine the chopped chocolate, corn syrup, and whipping cream. Stir until the chocolate is melted and smooth. Remove from the heat and stir in the brandy or liqueur. Pour into a serving bowl and serve with the chilled fruits and toothpicks.

VARIATION

You can also use small cookies for dipping as well as, or instead of, the pieces of fruit.

Shrimp Toasts

These crunchy sesame-topped toasts are simple to prepare using a food processor for the shrimp paste.

Makes 64

INGREDIENTS
8 ounces cooked, shelled shrimp, well drained and dried
1 egg white
2 green onions, chopped
1 teaspoon chopped fresh root ginger
1 garlic clove, chopped
1 teaspoon cornstarch
½ teaspoon salt
½ teaspoon sugar
2 to 3 dashes hot-pepper sauce
8 slices firm-textured white bread
4 to 5 tablespoons sesame seeds
vegetable oil for frying
green onion pompom, to garnish

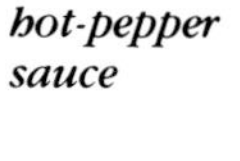

1 Put the first 9 ingredients in the bowl of a food processor and process until the mixture forms a smooth paste, scraping down the side of the bowl occasionally.

2 Spread the shrimp paste evenly over the bread slices, then sprinkle over the sesame seeds, pressing to make them stick. Remove the crusts, then cut each slice diagonally into 4 triangles, then cut each in half again to make 64 in total.

3 Heat 2 inches vegetable oil in a heavy saucepan or wok, until hot but not smoking. Fry the shrimp-coated triangles for 30 to 60 seconds, turning once. Drain on paper towels and serve hot.

COOK'S TIP

You can prepare these in advance and heat them up in a hot oven before serving. Make sure they are crisp and properly heated through though; they won't be nearly as enjoyable if there isn't any crunch!

Thai-Fried Vegetables in Wonton Cups

These crispy cups are an ideal way to serve stir-fried vegetables; use your imagination to vary the fillings.

Makes 24

INGREDIENTS

2 tablespoons vegetable oil, plus extra for greasing
24 small wonton wrappers
½ cup hoisin sauce or plum sauce (optional)
1 teaspoon sesame oil
1 garlic clove, finely chopped
½/inch piece fresh gingerroot, finely chopped
2-inch piece of lemongrass, crushed
6 to 8 asparagus spears, cut into 1¼-inch pieces
8 to 10 ears baby corn, cut in half lengthwise
1 small red pepper, seeded and cut into short slivers
1 to 2 tablespoons sugar
2 tablespoons soy sauce
juice of 1 lime
1 to 2 teaspoons Chinese-style chili sauce (or to taste)
1 tsp *nuac nam* or Thai or other fish sauce

1 Preheat the oven to 350°F. Lightly grease twenty-four 1½-inch muffin cups. Press one wonton wrapper into each cup, turning the edges up to form a cup shape. Bake for 8 to 10 minutes until crisp and golden. Carefully remove to a wire rack to cool. If you like, brush each cup with a little hoisin or plum sauce (this will help keep the cups crisp if preparing them in advance).

2 In a wok or large skillet, heat 2 tablespoons vegetable oil and the sesame oil until very hot. Add the garlic, ginger, and lemongrass and stir-fry for 15 seconds until fragrant. Add the asparagus, corn, and red pepper pieces and stir-fry for 2 minutes until tender crisp.

3 Add the sugar, soy sauce, lime juice, chili sauce, and fish sauce and toss well to coat. Stir-fry for 30 seconds longer.

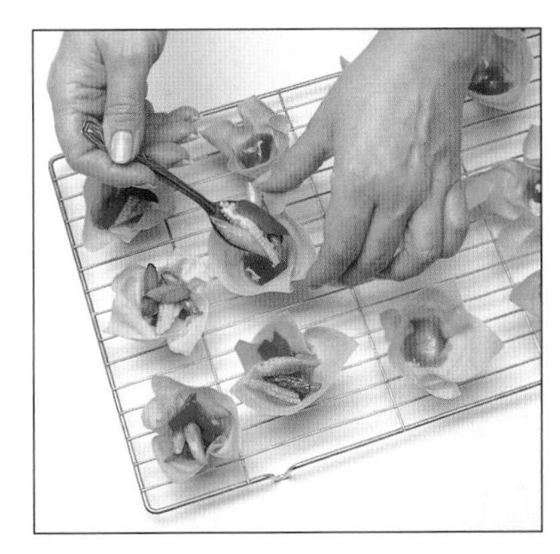

4 Spoon an equal amount of vegetable mixture into each of the prepared wonton cups and serve hot.

Chicken Satay with Peanut Sauce

These skewers of marinated chicken can be prepared in advance and served at room temperature. Beef, pork, or even lamb tenderloin can be used instead of chicken, if you prefer.

Makes about 24

INGREDIENTS
1 pound boneless, skinless chicken breast halves
sesame seeds, for sprinkling
red pepper, to garnish

FOR THE MARINADE
6 tablespoons vegetable oil
4 tablespoons tamari or light soy sauce
4 tablespoons fresh lime juice
½-inch piece fresh gingerroot, peeled and chopped
3 or 4 garlic cloves
2 tablespoons light brown sugar
1 teaspoon Chinese-style chili sauce, or 1 small red chili pepper, seeded and chopped
2 tablespoons chopped fresh cilantro

FOR THE PEANUT SAUCE
2 tablespoons smooth peanut butter
2 tablespoons soy sauce
1 tablespoon sesame or vegetable oil
2 green onions, chopped
2 garlic cloves
1 to 2 tablespoons fresh lime or lemon juice
1 tablespoon brown sugar

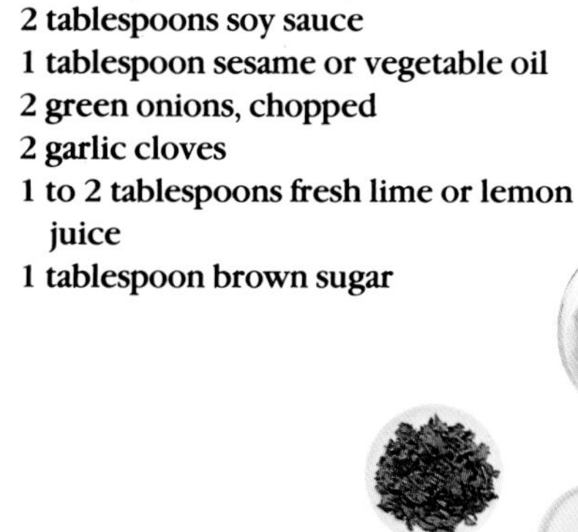

1 Prepare the marinade. Place all the marinade ingredients in the bowl of a food processor or blender and process until smooth and well blended, scraping down the sides of the bowl once. Pour into a shallow dish and set aside.

2 Into the same food processor or blender, put all the Peanut Sauce ingredients and process until well blended. If the sauce is too thick, add a little water and process again. Pour into a small bowl and cover until ready to serve.

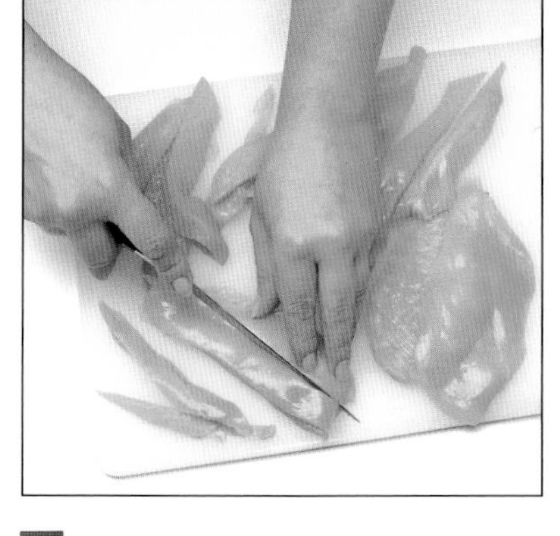

3 Put the chicken breast halves in the freezer for 5 minutes to firm. Slice the meat in half horizontally, then into thin strips. Cut the strips into ¾-inch pieces.

4 Add the chicken pieces to the marinade in the dish. Toss well to coat, cover and marinate for 3 to 4 hours in a cool place, or overnight in a refrigerator.

5 Preheat the broiler. Line a cookie sheet with foil and brush lightly with oil. Thread 2 to 3 pieces of marinated chicken onto skewers and sprinkle with the sesame seeds. Broil for 4 to 5 minutes until golden, turning once. Serve with the Peanut Sauce, and a garnish of red pepper strips.

COOK'S TIP

When using metal skewers, look for flat ones which prevent the food from spinning around. If using wooden skewers, be sure to soak them in cold water for at least 30 minutes, to prevent them burning.

Lamb Tikka

Creamy yogurt and nuts go wonderfully with the spices in these little Indian meatballs.

Makes about 20

INGREDIENTS
1 pound lamb tenderloin
2 green onions, chopped

FOR THE MARINADE
1 ½ cups plain yogurt
1 tablespoon ground blanched almonds, cashews, or peanuts
1 tablespoon vegetable oil
2 or 3 garlic cloves, finely chopped
juice of 1 lemon
1 teaspoon garam masala or curry powder
½ teaspoon ground cardamom
¼ teaspoon cayenne pepper
1 to 2 tablespoons chopped fresh mint

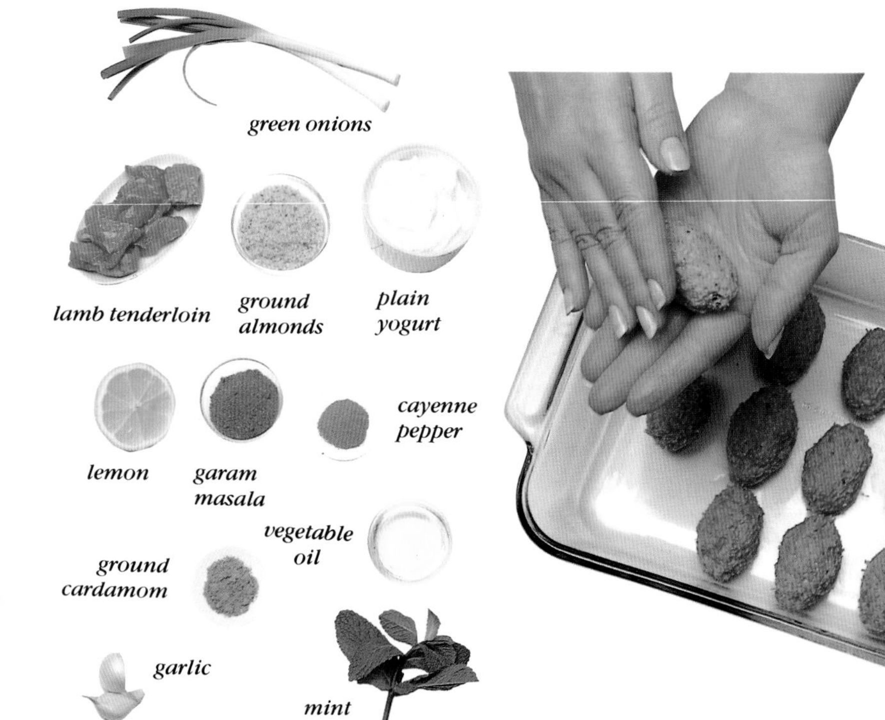

1 Prepare the marinade. In a medium-size bowl, stir together all the ingredients except the lamb. In a separate small bowl, reserve about ½ cup of the mixture to use as a dipping sauce.

2 Cut the lamb into small pieces and put in the bowl of a food processor with the green onions. Process, using the pulse action until the meat is finely chopped. Add 2 to 3 tablespoons of the marinade and process again.

3 Test to see if the mixture holds together by pinching a little between your fingertips. Add a little more marinade if necessary, but do not make the mixture too wet and soft.

4 With moistened palms, form the meat mixture into slightly oval-shaped balls about 1 ½ inches long and arrange in a shallow baking dish. Spoon over the remaining marinade, cover, and refrigerate the meatballs for 8 to 10 hours, or overnight.

5 Preheat the broiler and line a cookie sheet with foil. Thread each meatball onto a skewer and arrange on the cookie sheet. Broil for 4 to 5 minutes, turning occasionally, until crisp and golden on all sides. Serve with the reserved marinade/dipping sauce.

Smoked Duck Wontons with Spicy Mango Sauce

These Chinese-style wontons are easy to make using cooked smoked duck or chicken, or even left-over meat from Sunday lunch.

Makes about 40

INGREDIENTS
1 tablespoon light soy sauce
1 teaspoon sesame oil
2 green onions, finely chopped
grated peel of ½ orange
1 teaspoon brown sugar
1½ cups chopped smoked duck
about 40 small wonton wrappers
1 tablespoon vegetable oil

FOR THE SPICY MANGO SAUCE
2 tablespoons vegetable oil
1 teaspoon ground cumin
½ teaspoon ground cardamom
¼ teaspoon ground cinnamon
1 cup mango purée (about 1 large mango)
1 tablespoon honey
½ teaspoon Chinese chili sauce (or to taste)
1 tablespoon cider vinegar
snipped fresh chives, to garnish (optional)

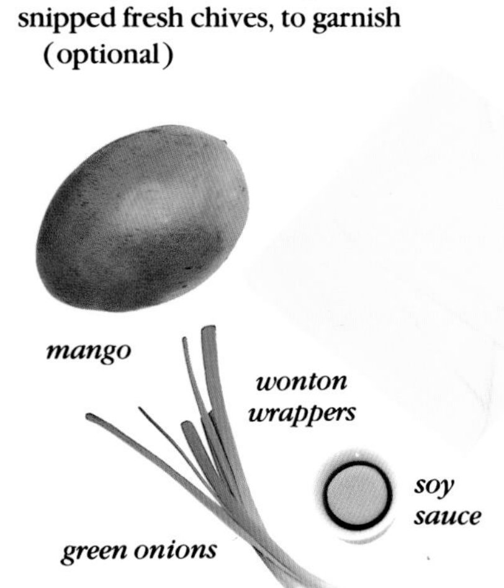

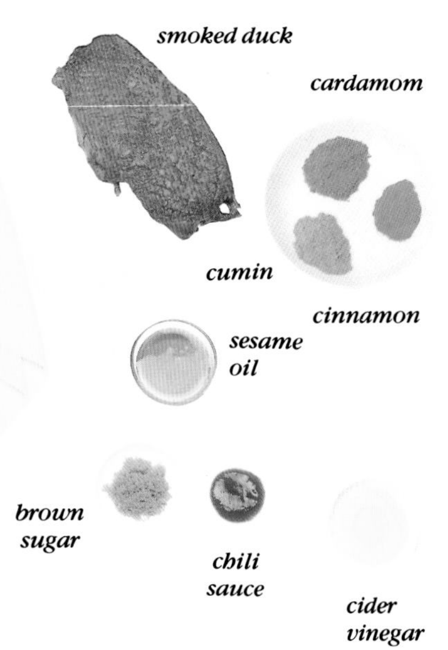

COOK'S TIP

Wonton wrappers, available in some large supermarkets and Asian markets, can be stored in the freezer almost indefinitely. Remove as many as you need, keeping the remainder frozen.

1 Prepare the sauce. In a medium-size saucepan, heat the oil over medium-low heat. Add the spices and cook for about 3 minutes, stirring constantly.

2 Stir in the mango purée, honey, chili sauce, and vinegar. Remove from the heat and cool. Pour into a bowl and cover until ready to serve.

3 Prepare the wonton filling. In a large bowl, mix together the soy sauce, sesame oil, green onions, orange peel, and brown sugar until well blended. Add the duck and toss to coat well.

4 Place a teaspoonful of the duck mixture in the center of each wonton wrapper. Brush the edges lightly with water and then draw them up to the center, twisting to seal and forming a pouch shape.

5 Preheat the oven to 375°C. Line a large cookie sheet with foil and brush lightly with oil. Arrange the wontons on the cookie sheet and bake for 10 to 12 minutes until crisp and golden. Serve with the Spicy Mango Sauce. If you wish, tie each wonton with a fresh chive.

Tandoori Chicken Sticks

This aromatic chicken dish is traditionally baked in a special clay oven called a *tandoor.*

Makes about 25

Ingredients
1 pound boneless, skinless chicken breast halves

For the Cilantro Yogurt
1 cup plain yogurt
2 tablespoons whipping cream
½ cucumber, peeled, seeded and finely chopped
1 to 2 tablespoons chopped fresh cilantro or mint
salt and freshly ground black pepper

For the marinade
¾ cup plain yogurt
1 teaspoon garam masala or curry powder
¼ teaspoon ground cumin
¼ teaspoon ground cilantro
¼ teaspoon cayenne pepper (or to taste)
1 teaspoon tomato paste
1 or 2 garlic cloves, finely chopped
½-inch piece fresh gingerroot, peeled and finely chopped
grated peel and juice of ½ lemon
1 to 2 tablespoons chopped fresh cilantro or mint

1 Prepare the Cilantro Yogurt. Combine all the ingredients in a bowl and season with salt and freshly ground black pepper. Cover and refrigerate until ready to serve.

2 Prepare the marinade. Place all the ingredients in the bowl of a food processor and process until smooth. Pour into a shallow dish.

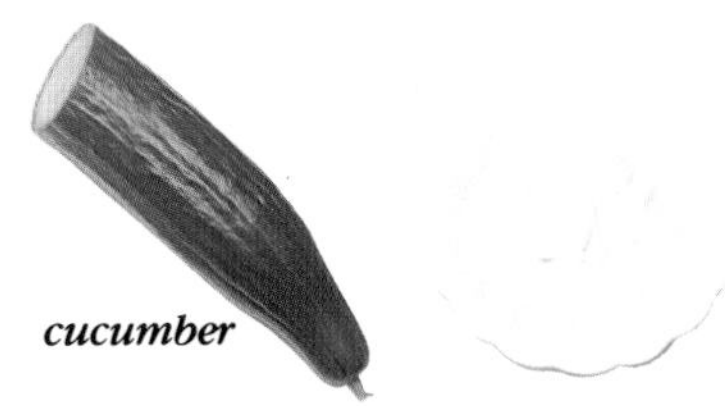

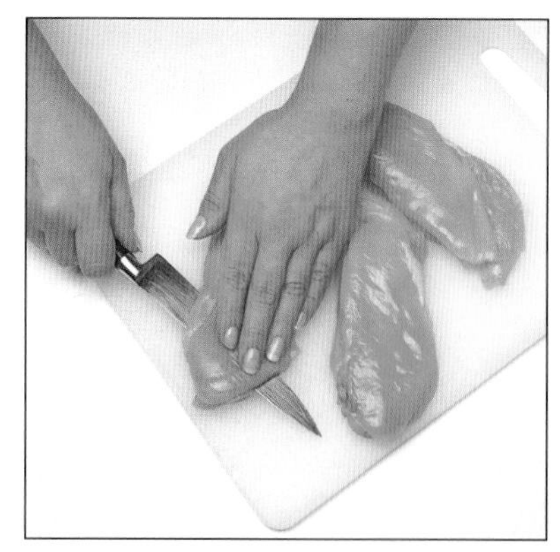

3 Freeze the chicken breasts for 5 minutes to firm, then slice in half horizontally. Cut the slices into ¾-inch strips and add to the marinade. Toss to coat well. Cover and refrigerate for 6 to 8 hours, or overnight.

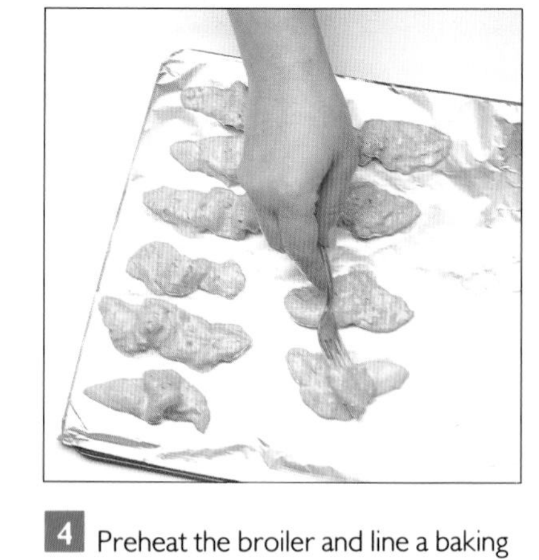

4 Preheat the broiler and line a baking sheet with foil. Using a slotted spoon, remove the chicken from the marinade and arrange the pieces in a single layer on the baking sheet. Scrunch up the chicken slightly so it makes wavy shapes. Grill for 4 to 5 minutes until brown and just cooked, turning once. Thread 1 or 2 pieces on to toothpicks or short skewers and serve with the yogurt dip.

Glazed Spareribs

These delicious sticky ribs are easy to eat with fingers once the little bones are cleaned away at one end to provide "handles."

Makes about 25

INGREDIENTS

- 2¼ pounds meaty pork spareribs, cut into 2-inch pieces
- ¾ cup tomato ketchup or mild chili sauce
- 2 to 3 tablespoons soy sauce
- 2 to 3 tablespoons honey
- 2 garlic cloves, finely chopped
- ¼ cup orange juice
- ¼ teaspoon cayenne pepper (or to taste)
- ¼ teaspoon Chinese five-spice powder
- 1 or 2 star anise

1 Using a small sharp knife, scrape away about ¼ inch of meat from one end of each tiny sparerib to serve as a little "handle."

2 In a large bowl or shallow baking dish, mix together the ketchup or chili sauce, soy sauce, honey, garlic, orange juice, cayenne pepper, Chinese five-spice powder, and star anise until well blended. Add the ribs and toss to coat. Cover and refrigerate for 6 to 8 hours, or overnight.

3 Preheat the oven to 350°F. Line a baking tray with foil and arrange the spareribs in a single layer, spooning over any remaining marinade.

4 Bake, uncovered, basting occasionally, for 1 to 1½ hours, or until the ribs are well browned and glazed. Serve warm or at room temperature.

Sushi-style Tuna Cubes

These tasty tuna cubes are easier to prepare than classic Japanese sushi but retain the same fresh taste.

Makes about 24

Ingredients
- 1½ pounds fresh tuna steak, ¾-inch thick
- 1 large red pepper, seeded and cut into ¾-inch pieces
- sesame seeds for sprinkling

For the marinade
- 1 to 2 tablespoons lemon juice
- ½ teaspoon salt
- ½ teaspoon sugar
- ½ teaspoon wasabi paste
- ½ cup olive or vegetable oil

For the Soy Dipping Sauce
- ½ cup soy sauce
- 1 tablespoon rice wine vinegar
- 1 teaspoon lemon juice
- 1 or 2 green onions, finely chopped
- 1 teaspoon sugar
- 2 to 3 dashes Asian hot chili oil or hot-pepper sauce

1 Cut the tuna into 1-inch pieces and arrange them in a single layer in a large noncorrosive baking dish.

2 Prepare the marinade. In a small bowl, stir the lemon juice with the salt, sugar, and wasabi paste. Slowly whisk in the oil until well blended and slightly

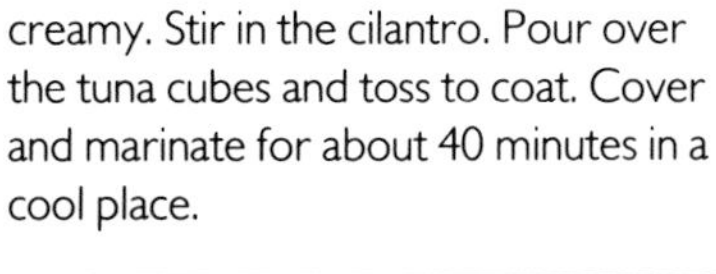
creamy. Stir in the cilantro. Pour over the tuna cubes and toss to coat. Cover and marinate for about 40 minutes in a cool place.

3 Meanwhile, prepare the Soy Dipping Sauce. Combine all the ingredients in a small bowl and stir until well blended. Cover until ready to serve.

4 Preheat the broiler and line a cookie sheet with foil. Thread a cube of tuna and then a piece of pepper onto each skewer and arrange on the cookie sheet.

5 Sprinkle with sesame seeds and broil for 3 to 5 minutes, turning once or twice, until just beginning to color but still pink inside. Serve with the Soy Dipping Sauce.

Cook's Tip

Wasabi is a hot, pungent Japanese horseradish available in powder form and as paste in a tube from gourmet and Japanese food stores.

Bombay Shrimp

These larger shrimp are expensive, so save this dish for a special occasion.

Makes 24

INGREDIENTS
¾ cup olive oil
1 teaspoon ground turmeric (or to taste)
1 teaspoon ground cumin
1 teaspoon garam masala or curry powder
½ teaspoon salt
½ teaspoon cayenne pepper (or to taste)
juice of 2 limes
24 large uncooked tiger or jumbo shrimp, shelled and deveined, tails attached
cilantro leaves, to garnish

1 In a medium-sized bowl, whisk together well the oil, turmeric, cumin, garam masala, salt, cayenne pepper, and lime juice.

2 With a small sharp knife, slit three-quarters of the way through each shrimp, cutting down the center back (be careful not to cut right through). Add the shrimp to the marinade and allow to stand in a cool place for 40 minutes.

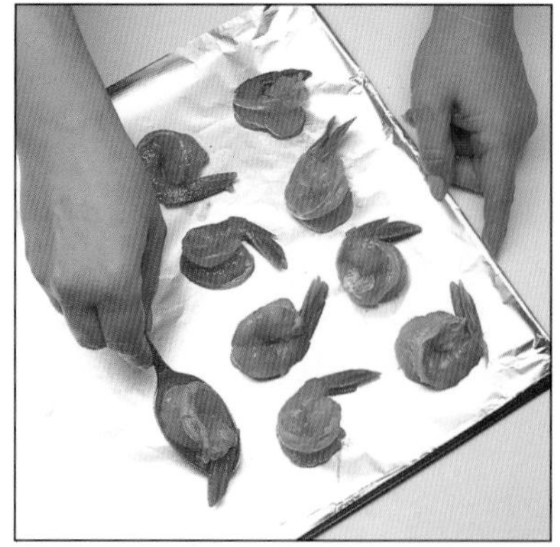

3 Preheat the broiler. Arrange the shrimp on a foil-lined broiler pan in a single layer. Drizzle a little of the marinade over. Broil for about 2 to 3 minutes until the shrimp are glazed and curled. Serve immediately, on toothpicks if you like, garnished with cilantro leaves.

COOK'S TIP

Wrap the shrimp tails in small pieces of foil to prevent them catching and burning under the broiler, then remove halfway through broiling. Make sure the shrimp are cooked through; test one by cutting in half.

Caramel Cape Gooseberries

These exotic fruits resemble shiny Chinese lanterns when dipped in golden caramel. Their tartness provides a perfect contrast to the sweetness of the coating.

Makes 24

INGREDIENTS
oil for greasing
24 Cape gooseberries
generous 1 cup granulated sugar
water

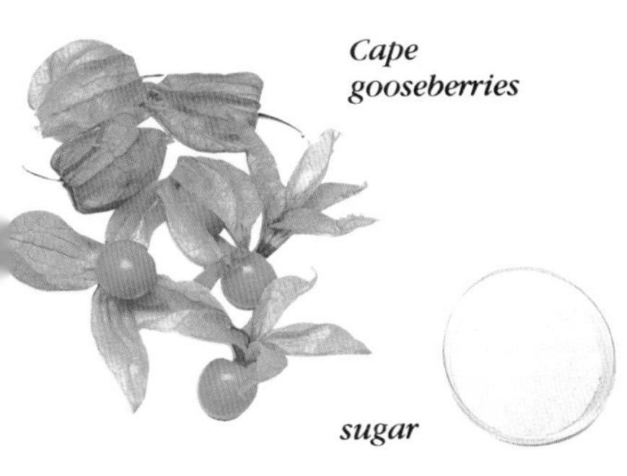

Cape gooseberries

sugar

1 Lightly oil a small cookie sheet. Carefully separate the papery leaves from the fruit of the Cape gooseberry and bend them back behind the berry, twisting them together at the stem.

2 Put the sugar in a small, heavy-bottomed saucepan, sprinkle with 2 to 3 tablespoons water and heat over low heat until the sugar melts, swirling the pan occasionally. Increase the heat to medium and bring to a boil. Boil for 4 to 5 minutes until the syrup turns a golden caramel color.

3 Dip the base of the pan in cold water to stop the cooking, then place it in a bowl of warm water so the caramel remains liquid. Be very careful, as the caramel can cause serious burns.

4 Holding each fruit by the papery leaves, carefully dip the berry into the caramel to coat completely. Set each fruit on the prepared baking sheet and allow to cool until hard.

Cocktails

The true origin of the first cocktails is uncertain, but without doubt it was in America that these "mixed drinks" gained the greatest popularity and where many of the more recent cocktail bar favorites were concocted. Cocktails developed in America with bourbon, Southern Comfort and Canadian rye whisky vying for attention. Prohibition was intended to curb drinking habits but only resulted in people ingeniously distilling their own liquors, which were softened by the addition of mixers.

Chic and classic with a strong American twist, the Harvey Wallbanger, the Martini and the Manhattan are here to stay, but more recently, flamboyant tropical cocktails have proved popular. Coconut milk and exotic fruits are whizzed together to create long, frothy cocktails. These concoctions are easily recreated at home now that exotic ingredients are readily available from large supermarkets.

Traditionally, a cocktail is made from only two liquors or liqueurs and the bartender's worth is gauged by making them perfectly, with just enough zing, shaken or stirred to taste. As a general rule, the simpler cocktails and those that are served clear, are just stirred over ice, in a bar glass, before being strained into a serving glass. Drinks that contain fizzy liquids are never shaken, for the obvious, explosive reasons. Cocktails with large quantities of fruit juices, syrups or eggs are shaken over ice in a cocktail shaker; cocktails containing milk, cream, ice cream or coconut milk make wonderful frothy drinks when mixed in the blender.

"Bar speak" is something to get acquainted with: when a recipe calls for a dash of bitters, that means just a shake of the bottle, a squeeze of lemon rind does not mean the whole thing floating in the drink. The rind should be held over the glass and twisted in the fingers, so that the lemon oil drops into the cocktail: the rind is then discarded. "On the rocks" quite simply means served over ice, and "straight up" means served just as it is, in a chilled glass.

At home you can create cocktails with no more than a cocktail shaker, large glass jug, blender and a few essential ingredients such as bitters, plain sugar syrup, and, of course, a couple of bottles of your favourite liquor and liqueurs. Making cocktails is an enjoyable pastime, so make a drink, sit back and savor it!

Liquors, Wines and Cider

Many cocktails contain the same liquors but in different combinations or quantities, so with a small stock of different drinks, a variety of cocktails is possible. For the best results, use the best quality brands available.

Brandy
Brandy is a popular liquor, distilled from grape wines. There are blended brandies available from all over the world, but some of the better and more expensive brandies are French. The two main types of French brandy are: cognac and Armagnac. There is also a range of fruit brandies, or eaux-de-vie, such as peach, cherry and apricot, as well as Calvados, which is a French fruit brandy distilled from apple wine. The American equivalent is applejack. All are perfect for using in a variety of cocktails.

Champagne
Use *brut* (dry) champagne or *méthode champenoise* wines when making cocktails. You'll find that they keep their sparkle a lot longer. Some of the less expensive champagne-style supermarket wines, such as the Spanish Cava, are ideal for mixing with a variety of fruit purées, freshly squeezed fruit juices and syrups.

Cider
A drink made from fermented apple juice. Sweet or dry cider both mix well with brandy and other spirits, as does perry, a cider made with pears. Use perry in exactly the same way as apple cider to make a tasty variation.

Gin
Gin is a favorite liquor and is ideal for mixing with many fruit juices and liqueurs, to create some of the classic cocktails. This colorless liquor is distilled from malted barley, rye or maize. Each brand uses its own very special combination of herbs, spices and citrus oils. Juniper berries give them all their most distinctive "gin" flavor.

Ginger Wine
A golden or green wine flavored, with citrus fruits, floral scents, herbs and ginger. It is sweet but very aromatic and spicy tasting and mixes well with liquors and red wine.

Marsala
This is a delicious fortified dessert wine from Sicily. It is a blend of white wine and brandy and has a sweet caramel flavor. Most people are familiar with sweet Marsala, but are unaware that a dry version with a flavor very similar to sherry can also be bought.

Port
A full-bodied wine, fortified with brandy during fermentation. It comes from the Douro valley of Portugal and is most commonly available as tawny, ruby, white, or Late Bottled Vintage (LBV).

Rum
Distilled from sugarcane and molasses and made mostly in the West Indies, particularly Jamaica, rum is available as dark or light varieties, as well as flavored with coconut and pineapple. It is used in cocktails such as the flamboyant Blue Hawaiian, Mai Tai and Planters Punch.

Schnapps
Generically known as aquavit, schnapps is a popular drink in Scandinavia and Germany. It is a colorless liquor made from grain starch and is also available in assorted fruit flavors such as peach, cherry, blackcurrant, pear and apple.

Sherry
This fortified wine originally came from Spain, but now it is also produced in a large number of other countries such as Greece, Cyprus, South Africa and Australia. It is available in a range of styles: *fino (*pale and dry), *manzanilla* (medium dry), *amontillado* (medium), *oloroso* and *amoroso* (sweetish) and *montilla* (lower in alcohol).

Tequila
Available in clear and golden (aged) hues, tequilas are fermented and distilled in Mexico, from the juice of the agave cactus. Tequila mixed with lime juice and a little salt is Mexico's national tipple. It is also an essential ingredient in the popular Margarita where it is mixed with Cointreau and lime.

Vermouth
A high-strength wine, cooked with a selection of herbs, vermouth is available as extra-dry white, bittersweet rosé, medium-sweet bianco and sweet red. By tradition, French vermouths are dry and Italian ones tend to have a sweeter flavor.

Vodka
A colorless liquor, distilled from rye, malt or potato starch, vodka originated in Eastern Europe. It has a completely neutral taste, which allows it to mix well with other liquors and fruit juices. Steeping vodka with fruits, fresh herbs and spices adds flavor and interest to the cocktail.

Whiskey
There are various types: Scotch whisky, Irish whiskey, the American bourbon and the Canadian rye. Whiskey is distilled from either malted or unmalted grains and can also be blended.

tequila
ginger wine
dark rum
champagne
light rum
sweet vermouth
Calvados
rsala
schnapps
cognac
vodka
whiskey
port
gin
fino sherry
dry vermou

Liqueurs

Many liqueurs available today originated as medicinal tonics, and a few were created by monks in their dispensaries. Liqueurs are made from a base liquor with herbs, peels of citrus fruit, spices or extracts from coffee beans.

Amaretto
A sweet Italian fruit-based liqueur with more than a hint of almonds and apricot, used in Hooded Claw and Cider Cup. It's made near the town of Saronno in Italy.

Anisette
Aniseed-flavored liqueurs like the Italian Sambuca and the Spanish anis are often flavored with coriander and fennel as well as aniseed. French Pernod and pastis are also anisettes, often served simply poured over plenty of ice cubes.

Benedictine
Made from an old French recipe passed down by the Benedictine monks of the abbey of Fécamp in Normandy, it is a golden colored, brandy-based liqueur, flavored with myrrh, other herbs and honey. It is an essential ingredient in the cocktail Sea Dog.

Chartreuse
A French brandy-based liqueur made from honey, herbs and spices. Originally made by Carthusian monks at La Grande Chartreuse monastery, the green liqueur has more alcohol than the yellow variety, which is flavored with oranges and myrtle.

Cointreau
Sweet and syrupy, it is a colorless liqueur with a strong aromatic orange flavor and is often served poured over ice.

Cream Liqueur
A mixture of cream, liquor and flavoring, such as Bailey's Irish Cream.

Crème de Cacao
A sweet liqueur originally made with cocoa beans from the Chouao region of Venezuela, it has a cocoa-vanilla flavor.

Crème de Cassis
A brandy-based blackcurrant liqueur produced in Dijon.

Crème de Menthe
A very sweet, peppermint-flavored liqueur, it also includes cinnamon, sage, ginger and orris and has strong digestive properties, which make it an ideal after-dinner drink.

Curaçao
An orange-flavored liqueur, similar to Grand Marnier, which was originally made from the dried peel of oranges from the island of Curaçao in the West Indies. It can be blue, as used in Blue Hawaiian, white or dark orange-brown in color.

Drambuie
A Scottish malt whisky-based liqueur, tinted with herbs, heather, honey and spices. Often used in after dinner coffee.

Galliano
A golden-colored herb liqueur, produced in Italy, and flavored with licorice and aniseed.

Grand Marnier
A French curaçao, based on extracts from the bitter bergamot, orange and brandy. It is similar to triple sec, curaçao and Cointreau.

Kahlúa
A rich, brown liqueur from Mexico. Although coffee-based like Tia Maria, Kahlúa is quite different in style and is popular in the USA.

Kümmel
This caraway and fennel-flavored liqueur is made mostly in Holland.

Southern Comfort
This American liqueur has a bourbon whiskey base and is flavored with fruit.

Tia Maria
A Jamaican liqueur made from rum, Blue Mountain coffee extract and spices. It can be used for a less sweet version of Kahlúa.

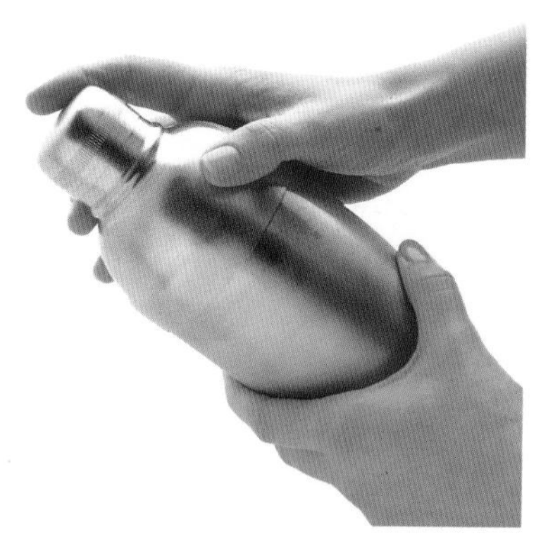

COOK'S TIP

Make sure your cocktail cabinet is stocked up with a few of these essentials.

Southern Comfort *Kahlúa* *Benedictine* *crème de menthe* *Grand Marnier* *Tia Maria* *Drambuie*

erry brandy *Galliano* *Crème de cacao* *Cointreau* *blue curaçao* *Anisette* *Amaretto* *Cream liqueur* *Green Chartreus*

Mixers and Juices

Whether a cocktail is shaken or simply stirred, it is the juices and mixers that provide a drink's length and body. After all, where would the Bloody Mary be without tomato juice?

These additions to the cocktail should always be as cold as possible. Juices are best if they are made from fresh fruit but, failing that, opt for the better quality, ready-squeezed versions which are not too sweet.

Apple Juice
Available still or sparkling and either clear or cloudy. Always choose a juice with little or no extra sugar or preservatives.

Bitter Lemon
A non-alcoholic fizzy mixer – good with all white liquors. It is made from carbonated water, lemon, sugar and quinine.

Coconut Milk
Used in tropical cocktails, unsweetened coconut milk is available in cans, or in a powdered form. The powder requires dissolving in hot water and then should be left to cool.

Cranberry Juice
A tangy and refreshing fruit drink, available in cartons and glass jars. The regular cranberry juice mixes well with spirits; other cranberry juices, mixed with raspberry or apple juice, offer further delicious flavor combinations.

Ginger Ale
Available in several varieties: dry, Canadian dry and the slightly

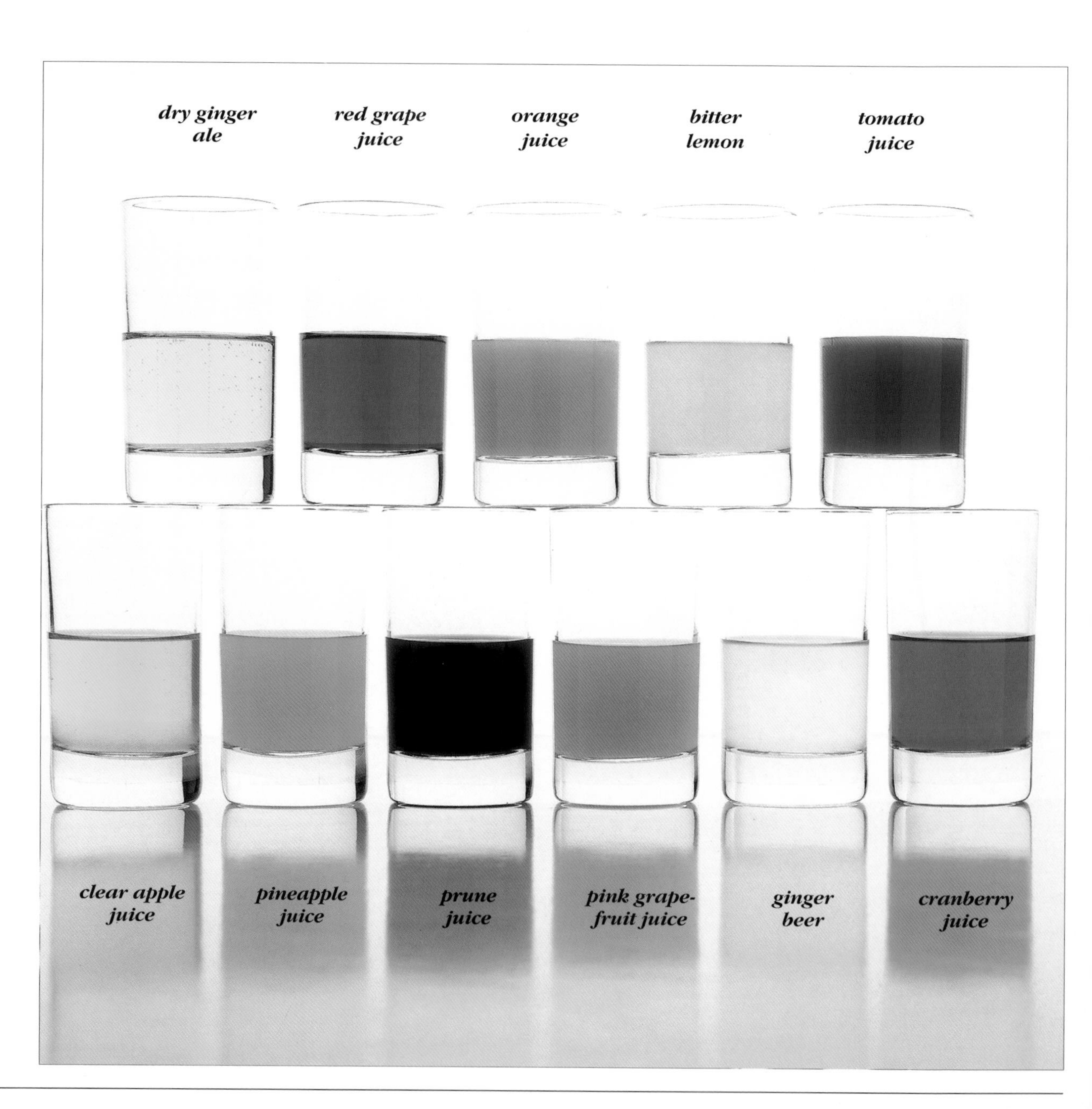

sweeter American dry. A non-alcoholic mixer, it is made from carbonated water, ginger extract and sugar. Mixes well with whiskey, bourbon and gin and is used in Kew Pimms.

Ginger Beer
A fermented drink made from ginger, sugar, water and yeast. The alcohol content in ginger beer is negligible.

Lemonade
Usually a non-alcoholic, fizzy soft drink although alcoholic varieties are now also available.

Orange Juice
For best results, either squeeze fresh oranges yourself or purchase chilled orange juice made from 100 percent fresh fruit. These have nothing added and no extra sugar. Other orange juices are mostly made with sweetened concentrates.

Passionfruit Cordial and Nectar
These are made with concentrated passionfruit juice and natural flavorings. The cordial is very strong and needs diluting to taste.

Pineapple Juice
The sweet and sour flavor of pineapple juice is imperative in many tropical cocktails. Use either freshly squeezed or out of a carton, and be sure to use the less sweet varieties.

Pink Grapefruit Juice
Often made from Florida pink grapefruits which are naturally sweet, it mixes well with white spirits. Look out for juices made from freshly squeezed fruit.

Prune Juice
This is produced in America and is made from a concentrate of dried prunes with no added sugar or preservatives.

Red Grape Juice
A light and fruity juice which is useful for making non-alcoholic cocktails. Choose cartons to keep in the cupboard and once opened, store in the fridge for no longer than three days.

Soda Water
A mixer containing sparkling water and bicarbonate of soda. Good to use when making long thirst-quenching cocktails. Sparkling mineral water or seltzer can be used in its place.

Tomato Juice
An excellent versatile mixer available in thick or thin consistencies. It can be found, mixed with clam juice, in a Canadian product called Clamato.

Tonic Water
A good old-fashioned mixer, which is used with gin, vodka or whiskey. Available in a low-calorie variety. It contains a small amount of quinine.

Added Flavors

These are the little extras that make all the difference between a good and a boring cocktail.

Bitters, Syrups and Sauces
The most widely used is angostura bitters, made in the West Indies from cloves, cinnamon, gentian, mace, nutmeg, quinine, prunes and other barks, stems and herbs. It has a distinctive flavor and rosy-red hue when a few drops are used. Grenadine and Rose's lime juice both add sweetness and hints of their own individual flavors of pomegranate and lime. Grenadine is also used for its pink/red color, which creates a glowing band at the bottom of a Mai-Tai and a Tequila Sunrise. Other herbs and spices are vital for their flavors and are used in making Tabasco sauce and Worcestershire sauce, both of which are used for maximum impact in a Bloody Mary. Balsamic and cider vinegars add a tart flavor but are less sour than lemon or lime juice.

Herbs
Ground celery seeds, fresh mint or lemon balm leaves and – during the summer months, fresh borage, chive or thyme flowers – add hints of aromatic flavors. These are used to great effect for their individual tastes and also for added color and decoration.

Spices
Freshly grated nutmeg, cloves, bruised cardamom pods, sticks of cinnamon and a pinch of cayenne, all pep up a basic punch or egg-nog; and freshly grated or creamed horseradish and fresh ginger add a zing all of their own to the simplest of juices. Use any spice with care, since an over-eager hand can easily upset the delicate balance of a cocktail. Taste the drink as you go and then add a little more if necessary.

Cocktail Equipment

To make a successful cocktail you need a few essential pieces of bartending equipment. The most vital and flamboyant is the cocktail shaker; what you have on hand in the kitchen can usually stand in for the rest. The equipment is listed below in descending order of importance.

Cocktail Shaker
Used for those drinks made with juices and syrups that need good mixing, but do not have to be crystal-clear. Cocktail shakers are usually made of stainless steel, silver, hard plastic or tough glass. The Boston shaker is made of two cup-type containers that fit over each other, one normally made of glass, the other of metal. This type is often preferred by professional bartenders. For beginners, the classic three-piece shaker is easier to handle, with its base to hold the ice and liquids, a top fitted with a built-in strainer and a tight-fitting cap.

Blender
Goblet blenders are the best shape for mixing cocktails that need to be aerated, to create a frothy cocktail or to be blended with finely crushed ice. A word of warning: do not be tempted to crush the ice in the blender, since this will blunt the blade. Opt for an ice bag or dish towel and a rolling pin and save your blender from ruin.

Ice Bag or Dish Towel
Essential for holding ice cubes when crushing, either to roughly cracked lumps or to a fine snow. The ice bag and towel must be scrupulously clean.

Wooden Hammer
For crushing the ice. The end of a wooden rolling pin also works just as well.

Short Glasses or Measuring Jug
For measuring out the required quantities. The measurements can be in single ($\frac{3}{4}$ oz) or double ($1\frac{1}{2}$ oz) bar measures or fluid ounces. Do not switch from one type of measurement to another. 1 measure equals $\frac{3}{4}$ oz/$1\frac{1}{2}$ tbsp.

Strainer
Used when pouring drinks from a shaker or bar glass to a cocktail glass. The best strainers are made from stainless steel and look like a flat spoon with holes and a curl of wire on the underside. These are held over the top of the glass to keep the fruit and ice back.

Mixing Pitcher or Bar Glass
It is useful to have a container in which to mix and stir drinks that are not shaken. The glass or pitcher should be large enough to hold two or three drinks. This vessel is intended for drinks that are meant to be clear, not cloudy.

Corkscrew
The fold-away type, with a can opener and bottle opener, is the most useful to have to hand.

Bar Spoon
These long-handled spoons can reach to the bottom of the tallest tumblers and are used for mixing the drink directly in the glass. Some varieties look like a large swizzle stick with a long handle and disk at one end.

Muddler
A long stick with a bulbous end, which is used for crushing sugar or mint leaves, and so is particularly useful when creating juleps. A variety of sizes is available. They are used like a pestle in a bar glass; the smaller version is used in an individual glass.

Lemon Knife and Squeezer
Citrus fruit is essential in many cocktails; a good quality, sharp knife is required for cutting the fruit and the squeezer for extracting its juice. Although fruit juice presses are quicker to use, they are more expensive.

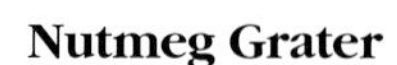

Nutmeg Grater
A tiny grater with small holes, for grating this hard nut over egg-nogs and frothy drinks.

Straws, Swizzle Sticks and Toothpicks
Used for the finishing decorative touches that complete a cocktail.

Zester and Canelle Knife
For presenting fruit when garnishing glasses. If you do not already have these, do not run out and buy them, since drinks can look equally attractive with simply sliced fruit.

Right: *1: blender; 2: cocktail shakers; 3: fruit juice press; 4: wooden hammer; 5: canelle knife; 6: corkscrew; 7: bar spoon; 8: strainer; 9: drinking straws; 10: shot glasses; 11: measuring spoons; 12: cup measures; 13: toothpicks; 14: swizzle sticks; 15: nutmeg grater; 16: cloth; 17: sharp knife.*

1
2
3
4
5
6
7
8
9
10
11
12
13
14
15
16
17

Glasses

Glasses should always be washed and dried with a glass cloth to ensure they are sparkling clean. Although some recipes suggest chilled glasses, don't put the best crystal in the freezer; leave it at the back of the refrigerator instead.

Cocktail or Martini Glass
This elegant glass is a wide conical bowl on a tall stem; a design which keeps cocktails cool by keeping warm hands away from the drink. It holds about ½ cup.

Collins Glass
The tallest of the tumblers, narrow with perfectly straight sides, it holds about 1 cup and is usually used for serving long drinks made with fresh juices or finished with soda.

Old-fashioned Glass
Classic, short whiskey tumblers are used for shorter drinks, which are served on the rocks. They hold about 6 oz.

Highball Glass
The middle-sized tumbler and the most frequently used glass. It holds about 8 oz.

Liqueur Glass
A tiny glass used to serve small measures of about 2 oz.

Brandy Balloon or Snifter
This glass is designed to trap the fragrance of the brandy in the bowl of the glass. Cupping the glass in the palms of the hands further helps to warm it gently and release its aromas.

Large Cocktail Goblets
These vary in size and shape and are used for serving larger frothy drinks, such as tropical cocktails like Piña Coladas. The wider rims of these glasses leave plenty of room for flamboyant, colorful decorations.

Champagne Glasses
Champagne can be poured into either attractive and old-fashioned champagne bowls or tall and slim flutes. The champagne flute is the more acceptable glass to use as it is more efficient at conserving the characteristic bubbles.

Red Wine Balloon
The most useful size of wine glass, holding 1 cup. It should only be filled halfway to allow the wine to be swirled around and release its bouquet.

White Wine Glass
This is a long-stemmed medium-sized glass that, once again, keeps warm hands away from the chilled wine or cocktail.

Pousse-café
A thin and narrow glass standing on a short stem. Used for floating or layered, stronger liqueur cocktails.

Above: *1: cocktail glass; 2: Collins glass; 3: old-fashioned glass; 4: highball glass; 5: liqueur glass; 6: brandy balloon; 7: large cocktail goblet; 8: champagne flute; 9: champagne bowl; 10: red wine balloon; 11: white wine glass; 12: pousse-café.*

Garnishes

It is far more eye-catching not to over-dress cocktails, otherwise all too quickly they turn into a fruit salad. Less is best! These edible extras add color, flavor and visual interest to any glass.

Frosting glasses with salt or sugar is a simple but effective touch, which hardly needs any extra decoration.

Edible garnishes should reflect the various contents of the cocktail. Citrus fruit is widely used because it is appetizing to look at and can be cut in advance and kept covered in the fridge, for a day, until required. Apple, pear and banana are suitable, but they do discolor on exposure to the air; dip them in lemon juice first to preserve color and flavor.

Fresh soft fruit such as strawberries, cherries, peaches, apricots and red currants make fabulous splashes of color and add a delicious flavor, but are only available in the summer.

The maraschino cherry is a popular option, and the endless supply of exotic fruits available all year long, such as mango, pineapple and star fruit, together offer numerous decorative ideas and combinations.

But not all garnishes and decorations need be fruit. Grated chocolate and nutmeg adorn egg-nogs and flips, while some Martinis call for a green olive – always opt for those packed in brine and not in oil. Plain or steeped-chili vodka can stand up to pickled chilies and the Gibson (a dry Martini) would not be a Gibson without a white pearl onion.

Crushing Ice

Some cocktails require cracked or crushed ice for adding to glasses, or a finely crushed ice "snow" for blending. It is not a good idea to crush ice in a blender or food processor as you may find it makes the blade blunt.

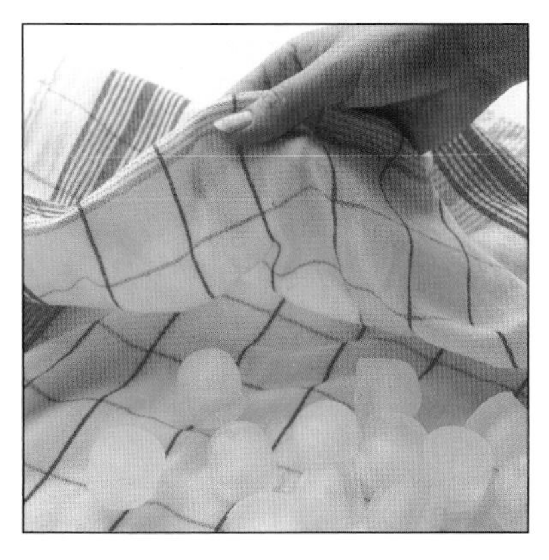

1 Lay a cloth on a work surface and cover half of the cloth with ice cubes. If you wish, you can use a cloth ice bag.

2 Fold the cloth over and, using the end of a rolling pin or a wooden mallet, strike the ice firmly several times, until you achieve the required fineness.

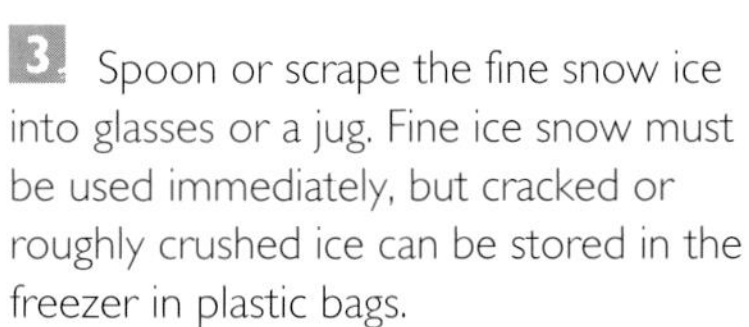

3 Spoon or scrape the fine snow ice into glasses or a jug. Fine ice snow must be used immediately, but cracked or roughly crushed ice can be stored in the freezer in plastic bags.

Making Decorative Ice Cubes

Decorative ice cubes can instantly jazz up simple cocktails. Flavor and color the cubes with fruit juices or bitters and freeze as normal.

1 Fill each compartment of an ice cube tray half-full with water and place in the freezer for 2–3 hours, or until the water has frozen.

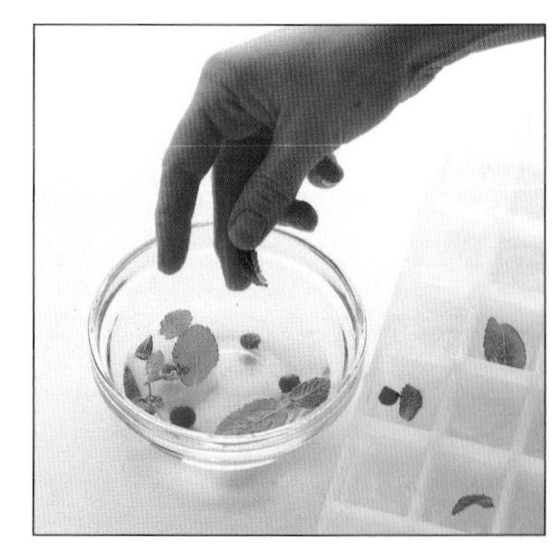

2 Prepare the fruit, olives, mint leaves, lemon rind, raisins or borage flowers and dip each briefly in water. Place in the ice-cube trays and freeze again.

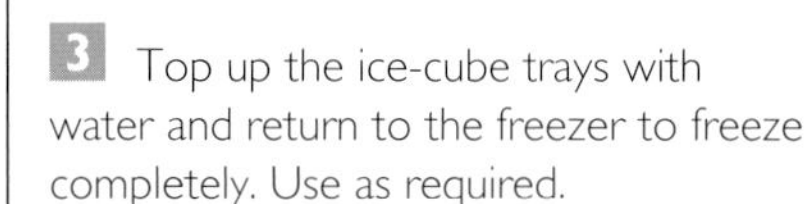

3 Top up the ice-cube trays with water and return to the freezer to freeze completely. Use as required.

Frosting Glasses

Frosting adds both to the appearance and taste of a cocktail. Use celery salt, grated coconut, grated chocolate, colored sugars or cocoa for an eye-catching effect. Once frosted, place the glass in the fridge to chill until needed.

1 Hold the glass upside down, so the juice does not run down the glass. Rub the rim of the glass with the cut surface of a lemon, lime, orange or even a slice of fresh pineapple.

2 Keeping the glass upside down, dip the rim into a shallow layer of sugar, coconut or salt. Redip the glass, if necessary, so the rim is well-coated.

3 Stand the glass upright and let it sit until the sugar, coconut or salt has dried on the rim, then chill.

Shaking Cocktails

Cocktails that contain sugar syrups or creams require more than just a stir; they are combined and chilled with a brief shake. Remember that it is possible to shake only one or two servings at a time, so you may have to work in batches.

1 Fill the cocktail shaker two-thirds full with ice cubes and pour in the spirits; add the mixers, if not sparkling, and the flavoring ingredients.

2 Put the lid on the shaker. Hold the shaker firmly in one hand, keeping the lid in place with the other hand.

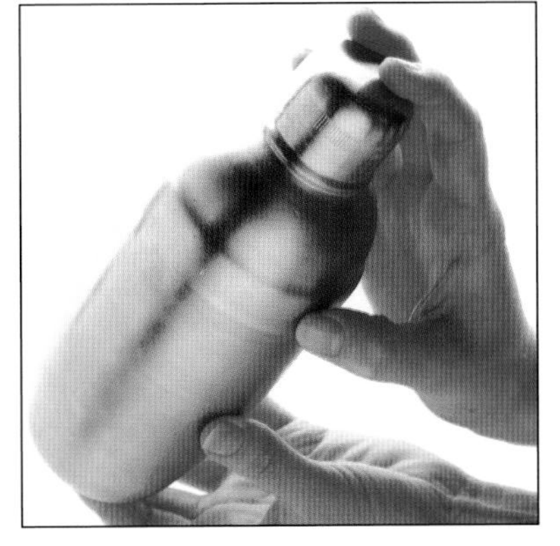

3 Shake vigorously, for about 10 seconds to blend simple concoctions and for 20–30 seconds for drinks with sugar syrups or eggs. By this time the shaker should feel cold.

4 Remove the small lid and pour into the prepared glass, using a strainer if the shaker is not already fitted with one.

Making Basic Sugar Syrup

A sugar syrup is sometimes preferable to sugar crystals for sweetening cocktails, since it immediately blends with the other ingredients.

Makes about 3 cups

INGREDIENTS
1½ cups sugar
2½ cups water

1 Place the sugar in a heavy-bottomed pan with the water, and heat gently over low heat. Stir with a wooden spoon until the sugar has dissolved.

2 Brush the sides of the pan with a pastry brush dampened in water to remove any sugar crystals that might cause the syrup to crystallize.

3 Bring to a boil for 3–5 minutes. Skim any scum and when no more appears, remove the pan from the heat.

4 Cool and pour into clean, dry, airtight bottles. Keep in the fridge for up to one month.

Making Flavored Syrup

Syrup can be flavored with anything: vanilla beans, mint or citrus peel. Just boil, then bottle with the syrup.

Makes about 1¼ cups

INGREDIENTS
2 pounds very ripe soft or stone fruit, washed
1 pound sugar

COOK'S TIP

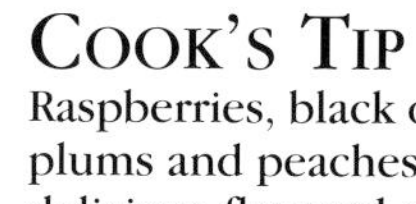

Raspberries, black or red currants, plums and peaches all make delicious flavored syrups.

1 Place the washed fruit of your choice in a bowl and, using the bottom of a rolling pin, a wooden pestle or a potato masher, crush the fruit to release the juices. Cover and allow to sit overnight to concentrate the flavor.

2 Strain the purée through a cloth bag or piece of muslin. Gather the corners of the cloth together and twist them tight, to remove as much juice as possible. Measure the amount of juice and add 8 oz sugar to every 1¼ cups fruit juice.

3 Place the pan over low heat and gently stir until all the sugar has dissolved. Continue as in the recipe for basic sugar syrup. The syrup will keep in the fridge for up to one month.

Making Flavored Liquors

Gin, vodka and white rum can be left to steep and absorb the flavors of a wide variety of soft fruits.

Makes 4 cups

Ingredients
1 pound raspberries, strawberries, or pineapple
1½ cups sugar
4 cups gin, vodka or light rum

Variations

Vodka and sliced bananas; white rum and fresh pineapple; gin and drained, canned lychees; sliced peaches or apricots; brandy and plums or apricots.

1 Place the fruit in a widemouth jar and add the sugar.

2 Add the liquor. Cover tightly. Leave in a cool, dark place for a month, shaking gently every week.

3 Strain through clean muslin or a cloth bag and squeeze out the rest of the liquid from the steeped fruit.

4 Return the flavored liquor to a clean bottle and seal, then store it in a cool, dark place.

Steeping Spirits

Steeping any spirit with a flavoring agent, such as chilies, creates a new sensation.

Makes 4 cups

Ingredients
4 cups sherry or vodka
½ cup small red chilies, or to taste

1 Wash and dry the chilies, discarding any that are less than perfect. Using a toothpick, prick the chilies all over to release their flavors.

2 Pack the chilies tightly into a sterilized bottle.

3 Top up with sherry or vodka. Fit the cork tightly and leave in a dark place for at least ten days or up to two months.

Variations

Try the following interesting alternatives: gin with cumin seeds, star anise or juniper berries; brandy with ½ cup peeled and sliced fresh ginger or ⅓ cup whole cloves; vodka with ½ cup washed raisins or 1–2 tablespoons cracked black peppercorns; rum with 2–3 pricked vanilla pods. The amount of flavoring used is a matter of personal taste.

Gin Smash

Try this cocktail with any fresh mint you can find: peppermint and spearmint would each contribute their own flavor to this simple and very refreshing cocktail.

VARIATION

Use Southern Comfort or bourbon in place of the gin.

Serves 1

INGREDIENTS
1 tablespoon sugar
4 sprigs fresh mint
2 measures/3 tablespoons dry gin

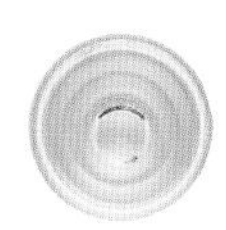

gin

sugar

mint

1 Dissolve the sugar in a little water in the cocktail shaker.

2 Place some ice cubes in a clean dish towel and crush them finely.

3 Add the mint to the cocktail shaker and, using a muddler, bruise and press the juices out of the leaves.

4 Half fill the shaker with the cracked ice and add the gin.

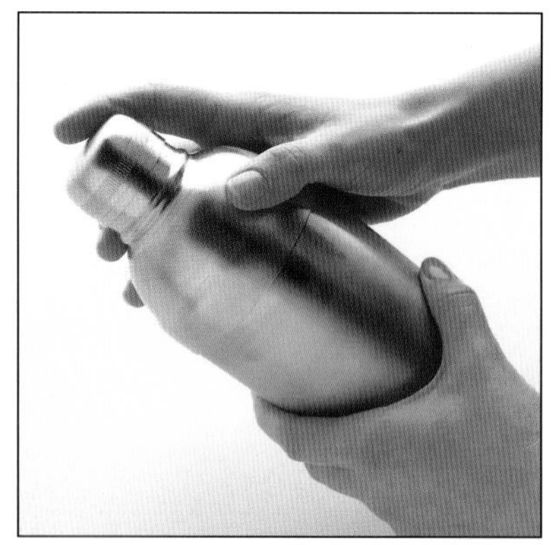

5 Secure the top of the shaker and shake the cocktail for about 20 seconds, to mix the gin with the mint.

6 Strain into a small wine glass filled with crushed ice. If desired, add fresh mint sprigs and drinking straws.

Gall Bracer

Short and smart, this drink is served on the rocks in a tumbler or in a long-stemmed glass with a maraschino cherry depending on the drinker and the occasion.

Serves 1

INGREDIENTS
2 dashes angostura bitters
2 dashes grenadine
2 measures/3 tablespoons whiskey
lemon rind
maraschino cherry, to decorate (optional)

grenadine

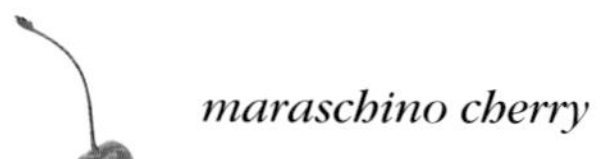

maraschino cherry

whiskey

angostura bitters

1 Half fill a bar glass with ice cubes. Add the angostura bitters, grenadine and whiskey and stir well to chill.

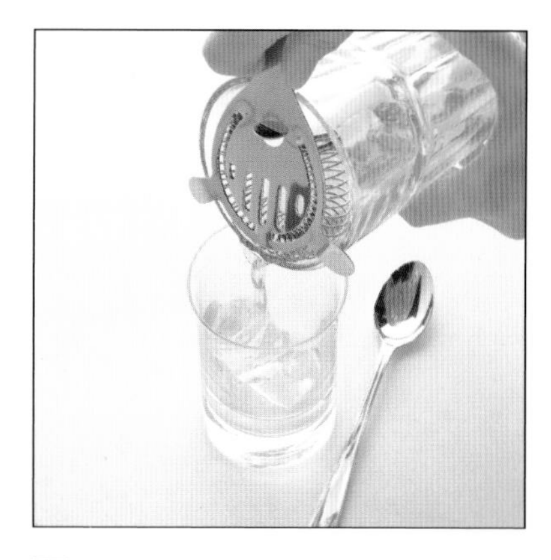

2 Place some ice in a short tumbler and pour the cocktail over it.

3 Holding the lemon rind between your fingers, squeeze out the oil and juices into the cocktail. Discard the lemon rind.

4 Decorate with a cherry, if desired.

VARIATION

For a longer drink, finish with soda or sparkling mineral water, or for a cocktail called a Gall Trembler, substitute gin for the whiskey and add more bitters.

Gibson

Well loved in Japan, this is a version of the Martini with a pearl onion, rather than the usual twist of lemon. You may prefer to use a higher proportion of gin.

Serves 1

INGREDIENTS
- $^{1}/_{2}$ measure/2 teaspoons extra-dry vermouth
- 1 scant measure/$1^{1}/_{4}$ tablespoons extra-dry gin
- 2 pearl onions, to decorate

extra-dry vermouth

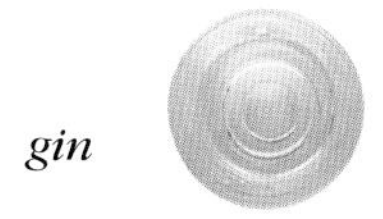
gin

pearl onions

VARIATION

Add a touch more dry vermouth and a twist of lemon and you have an Australian Kangaroo.

1 Pour the vermouth into a bar glass of ice, stir briskly and then pour out the liquid. Only the vermouth that clings to the ice and glass should be used.

2 Add the gin and stir for at least 30 seconds to chill well.

3 Strain into a martini glass, either on the rocks or straight up.

4 Thread the pearl onions onto a toothpick and add to the drink.

Brandy Alexander

A warming digestif, made from a blend of crème de cacao, brandy and double cream, that can be served at the end of the meal with coffee.

Serves 1

INGREDIENTS
- 1 measure/1½ tablespoons brandy
- 1 measure/1½ tablespoons crème de cacao
- 1 measure/1½ tablespoons heavy cream
- whole nutmeg, to decorate

crème de cacao

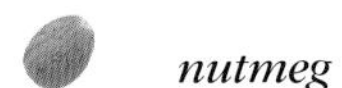
nutmeg

heavy cream

brandy

1 Half fill the cocktail shaker with ice and pour in the brandy, crème de cacao and the cream.

2 Shake for about 20 seconds to mix thoroughly.

3 Strain the chilled cocktail into a small wine glass.

4 Finely grate a little nutmeg over the top of the cocktail.

VARIATION
Warm the brandy and the heavy cream gently and add to a blender with the crème de cacao. Blend until frothy. Serve with a cinnamon stick.

Perfect Manhattan

When making Manhattans it's a matter of preference whether you use sweet vermouth, dry vermouth or a mixture of the two. Both of the former require a dash of angostura bitters.

Serves 1

INGREDIENTS
2 measures/3 tablespoons rye whiskey
1/4 measure/1 teaspoon dry vermouth
1/4 measure/1 teaspoon sweet vermouth
1 lemon
maraschino cherry, to decorate

sweet vermouth

maraschino cherry

whiskey

dry vermouth

lemon rind

1 Pour the whiskey and vermouths into a bar glass half full of ice. Stir well for 30 seconds to mix and chill.

2 Strain on the rocks or straight up into a chilled cocktail glass.

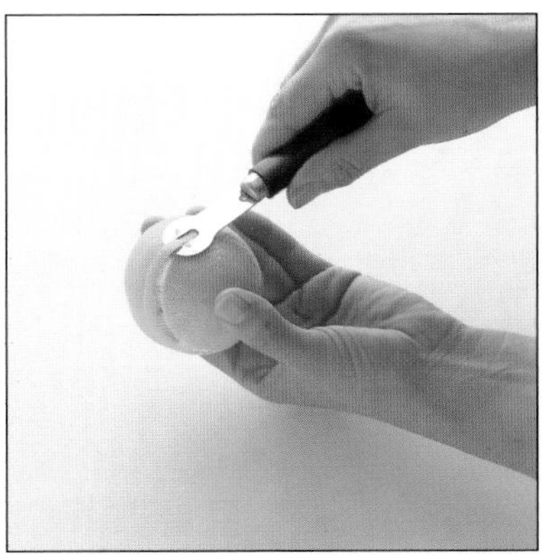

3 Using a canelle knife, pare away a small strip of lemon rind. Tie it into a knot to help release the oils from the rind, and drop it into the cocktail.

4 To finish, add a maraschino cherry with its stalk left intact.

VARIATION

Create a Skyscraper by adding a dash of angostura bitters, a teaspoon of maraschino cherry juice, and finish with ginger ale.

Margarita

Traditionally, this popular strong apéritif is made with tequila and Cointreau, but it is also good made with vodka and triple sec (an orange-flavored liqueur similar to white curaçao).

VARIATION

Replace the Cointreau with blue curaçao for a vivid color and a stimulating flavor.

Serves 1

INGREDIENTS

1 measure/1 1/2 tablespoons tequila
1 measure/1 1/2 tablespoons Cointreau
2/3 measure/1 tablespoon fresh lime juice
wedge of fresh lime, fine salt and cucumber, to decorate

tequila

salt

Cointreau

lime juice

cucumber peel

1 Rub the rim of the glass with a wedge of fresh lime.

2 Invert the glass into fine salt to create a rim of salt. Turn the glass the right way up and chill until required.

3 Pour the tequila and Cointreau, with the lime juice, into a cocktail shaker filled with ice. Shake for 20 seconds.

4 Carefully strain the cocktail into the frosted glass.

5 Using a sharp knife or vegetable peeler, cut a long thin strip of green peel from a whole cucumber.

6 Trim the cucumber peel to size and thread it onto a toothpick. Add to the glass to decorate.

Hooded Claw

Syrupy-sweet prune juice with Amaretto and Cointreau makes a delicious digestif when poured over finely crushed ice snow.

Serves 4

INGREDIENTS
5 measures/½ cup prune juice
2 measures/3 tablespoons Amaretto
1 measure/1½ tablespoons Cointreau

Amaretto

Cointreau

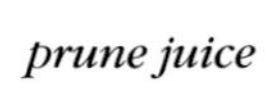

prune juice

1 Pour the prune juice, Amaretto and Cointreau into a cocktail shaker half filled with ice.

2 Shake the cocktail for 20 seconds to chill well.

3 Loosely fill four small liqueur glasses with finely crushed snow ice.

4 Strain the drink into the glasses and serve with short straws.

Bitter Gimlet

An old-fashioned apéritif, which could easily be turned into a longer drink by finishing it with chilled tonic or soda water.

Serves 1

INGREDIENTS
1 lime, cut into wedges
1 measure/1½ tablespoons gin
2 dashes angostura bitters
slice and rind of lime, to decorate

lime wedges

lime decoration

angostura bitters

gin

1 Place the lime at the bottom of the bar glass and, using a muddler, press the juice out of the lime.

2 Add cracked ice, the gin and the bitters and stir well until chilled.

3 Strain the cocktail into a short tumbler over ice cubes.

4 Add a triangle of lime rind to the drink and rest a slice of lime on the rim of the glass.

VARIATION

Add a teaspoon of sugar, for a sweeter version, or a dash or two of crème de menthe to create a Fallen Angel.

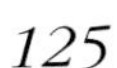

Chili Vodkatini

Not quite a Martini, but almost. Over the years, the proportions of vodka to vermouth have varied widely, with the vodka becoming almost overwhelming. Be sure to have your chili vodka made well in advance and ready to use.

Serves 1

INGREDIENTS

- 1 measure/1½ tablespoons chili vodka
- ¼ measure/1 teaspoon medium or dry French vermouth
- 2 small pickled or vodka-soaked chilies, to decorate
- 1 pitted green olive, to decorate

chili vodka

dry vermouth

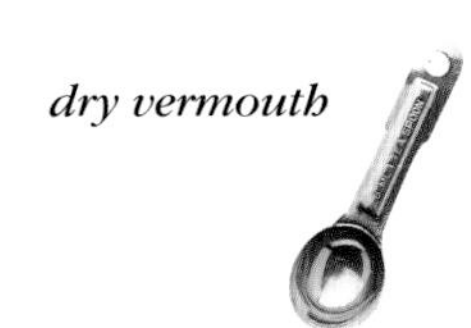

chili-stuffed olive

1 Add the chili vodka to a bar glass of ice and mix for about 30 seconds, until the outside of the glass is frosted over.

2 Add the vermouth to a chilled cocktail glass and swirl it around the inside of the glass to wet it. Discard any remaining vermouth.

3 Cut one of the pickled chilies in half and discard the seeds. Stuff the pitted green olive with the chili.

4 Thread the stuffed olive onto a toothpick with the remaining chili.

5 Strain the cocktail into the prepared cocktail glass.

6 Add the olive and chili decoration to the drink before serving.

VARIATION

For the classic Martini, use gin, but serve with a twist of lemon. Mix plain vodka and dry vermouth for a Vodka Martini. Add an olive and it becomes a Vodka Gibson.

Gin Crusta

Prepare the glass in advance and keep it chilled in the fridge ready for instant use! The depth of pink color will depend on the strength of the maraschino cherry juice you use.

VARIATION

Make in the same way with whiskey, Southern Comfort, brandy or rum.

Serves 1

INGREDIENTS
- 1 lemon
- 3 dashes sugar syrup
- 2 dashes maraschino cherry juice
- 2 dashes angostura bitters
- 1 measure/1½ tablespoons dry gin
- 2 tablespoons golden granulated sugar

angostura bitters

maraschino cherry juice

golden granulated sugar

lemon juice

gin

sugar syrup

lemon rind

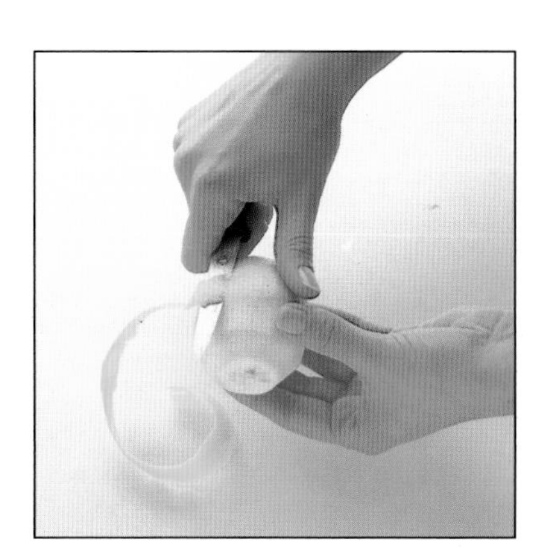

1 Cut both ends off the lemon and, using a paring knife or canelle knife, peel the lemon thinly, as you would an apple, in one long, continuous piece.

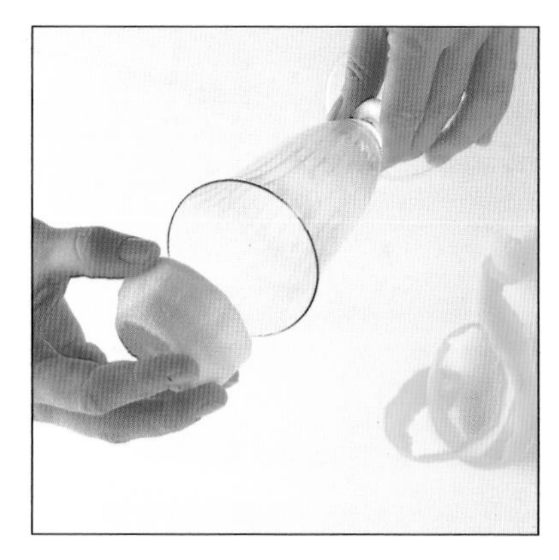

2 Halve the whole lemon and rub the edge of a glass with one half.

3 Turn the glass upside-down and dip it into the granulated sugar to create a decorative rim.

4 Arrange the lemon rind in a scroll on the inside of the glass.

5 Add the sugar syrup, maraschino cherry juice, angostura bitters, gin and juice of ¼ of the lemon to a cocktail shaker, half filled with ice.

6 Shake for about 30 seconds and carefully strain into the prepared glass.

Airstrike

A variation on a Val d'Isère Shooter, similar to the Italian Flaming Sambuca.

Serves 1

INGREDIENTS
2 measures/3 tablespoons Galliano
1 measure/$1^1/_2$ tablespoons brandy
1 star anise

Galliano

star anise

brandy

1 Put the Galliano and brandy in a small saucepan and heat very gently, until just warm.

2 Carefully pour into a heat-resistant glass standing on a small plate or saucer; add the star anise.

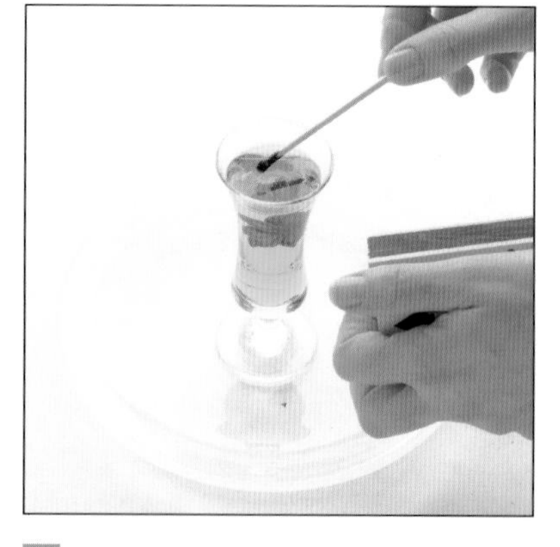

3 Using a lighted taper or long match, pass the flame over the surface of the drink to ignite it. The flame will be low and very pale, so be careful not to burn yourself.

4 Let burn for a couple of minutes, until the star anise has sizzled a little and released its aroma into the drink. Cool slightly before drinking. Beware, the top of the glass will be hot!

VARIATION

Use only Sambuca and float two or three fresh coffee beans on the surface instead of the star anise before lighting.

B-52

This cocktail depends on the difference in specific weight or densities of each of the liqueurs to remain strictly separated in layers.

Serves 1

INGREDIENTS
1 measure/1½ tablespoons Kahlúa
1 measure/1½ tablespoons Grand Marnier
1 measure/1½ tablespoons Bailey's Irish Cream

Grand Marnier

Bailey's Irish Cream

Kahlúa

1 Pour the Kahlúa into a small shot glass or pousse-café.

2 Hold a cold teaspoon upside-down, just barely touching the surface of the Kahlúa and the side of the glass.

3 Slowly and carefully pour the Grand Marnier over the back of the teaspoon to create a second layer.

4 In the same way, carefully pour the Bailey's over the back of a second clean teaspoon to create a final layer. This layer in fact will form the middle layer and push the Grand Marnier to the top.

VARIATION

Create a similar effect with equal quantities of Bailey's, Kahlúa and vodka, layered in that order. Or try Chartreuse, cherry brandy and kümmel with cumin seeds floated on the top instead.

Coffee and Chocolate Flip

Since the egg is not cooked, use only the freshest eggs. For a hint of honey, substitute Drambuie for the brandy, but omit the sugar. Replace the Kahlúa with Tia Maria for a less sweet version.

Serves 1

INGREDIENTS
1 egg
1 tsp sugar
1 measure/1½ tablespoons brandy
1 measure/1½ tablespoons Kahlúa
1 tsp instant coffee granules
3 measures/4½ tablespoons heavy cream
cocoa powder or grated chocolate, to decorate

1 Separate the egg and lightly beat the white until frothy and white.

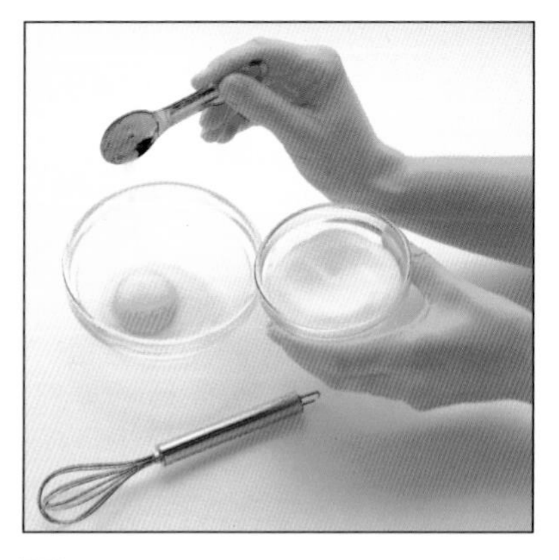

2 In a separate bowl, beat the egg yolk with the sugar.

3 In a small saucepan, combine the brandy, Kahlúa, coffee and cream and warm over very low heat.

4 Allow the mixture to cool, then whisk it into the egg yolk.

5 Add the egg white to the egg and cream and pour the mixture briefly back and forth between two glasses, until it is smooth.

6 Pour into a tall glass over coarsely crushed ice and sprinkle the top with cocoa powder.

VARIATION

Shake together equal quantities of Kahlúa, chocolate-flavored milk and coffee. Serve on the rocks.

Cranberry Kiss

A delicious full-flavored cocktail with the tang of cranberry and pink grapefruit juices and the sweetness of Marsala.

VARIATION

Shake cranberry and pineapple juice with unsweetened coconut milk. Add vodka or gin to taste.

Serves 1

INGREDIENTS

- 2 measures/3 tablespoons cranberry juice
- 1 measure/$1\frac{1}{2}$ tablespoons brandy
- 2 measures/3 tablespoons pink grapefruit juice
- 2 measures/3 tablespoons Marsala
- red currants, to decorate
- 1 egg white, lightly beaten, and 1 tablespoon sugar, to decorate

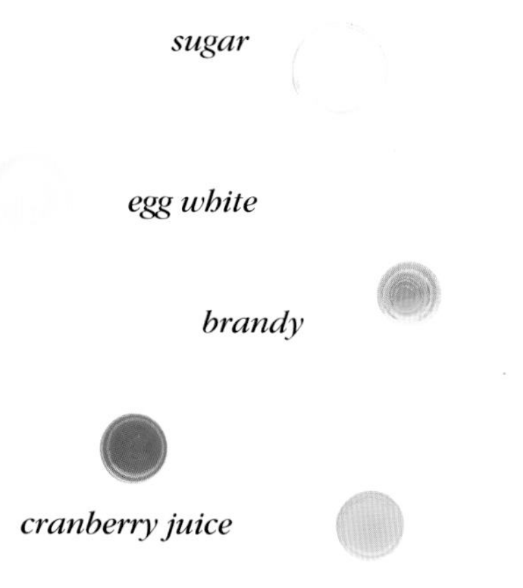

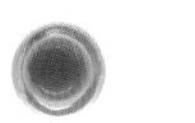

1 For the decoration, lightly brush the red currants with the egg white.

2 Shake sugar over the red currants, to cover with a frosting. Set aside to dry.

3 Add the cranberry juice, brandy and grapefruit juice to a cocktail shaker full of crushed ice and shake for 20 seconds.

4 Strain into a well chilled glass.

5 Tilt the glass slightly before slowly pouring in the Marsala down the side of the glass.

6 Serve, decorated with the frosted red currants.

Grasshopper

A minted, creamy cocktail in an attractive shade of green. If you use dark crème de cacao, the cocktail will not be as vibrant a color, but you'll find that it tastes just as good.

Serves 1

Ingredients

- 2 measures/3 tablespoons crème de menthe
- 2 measures/3 tablespoons light crème de cacao
- 2 measures/3 tablespoons heavy cream
- melted bittersweet chocolate, to decorate

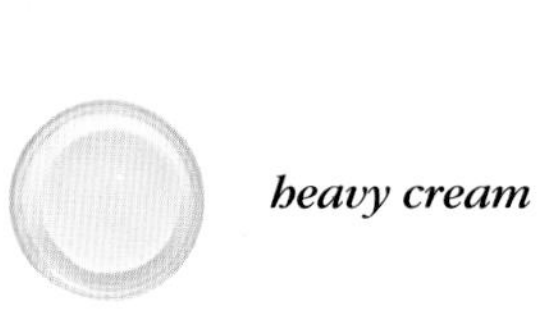

heavy cream

crème de menthe

crème de cacao

bittersweet chocolate

Variation

Mix in a blender with crushed ice for a smoother consistency. To make a Scandinavian Freeze, mix 2 measures each of vodka and crème de cacao and a scoop of vanilla ice cream and process until just smooth.

1 Pour the crème de menthe and crème de cacao into a cocktail shaker and add the cream.

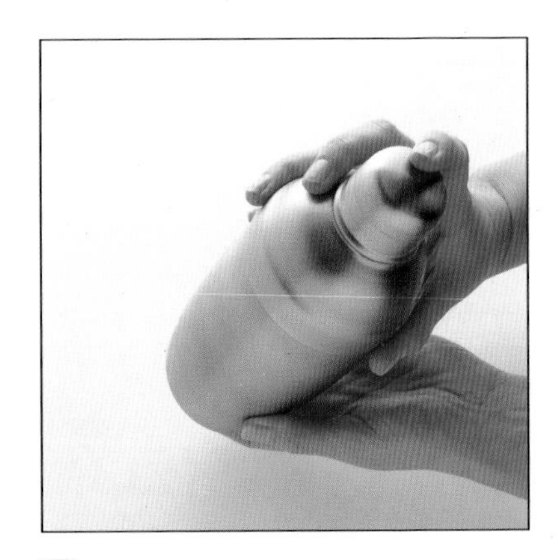

2 Add some cracked ice and shake well for 20 seconds.

3 Strain the cocktail into a tumbler of finely cracked ice.

4 To decorate, spread the melted chocolate evenly over a plastic board and leave to cool and harden. Draw the blade of a sharp knife across the chocolate to create curls. Add to the top of the cocktail.

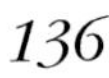

Tequila Sunset

This variation on the popular party drink can be mixed and chilled in a pitcher, ready to pour into glasses, and finished at the last minute with the addition of crème de cassis and honey.

Serves 1

INGREDIENTS

- 1 measure/1½ tablespoons clear or golden tequila
- 5 measures/½ cup fresh lemon juice, chilled
- 1 measure/1½ tablespoons orange juice, chilled
- 1–2 tablespoons clear honey
- ⅔ measure/1 tablespoon crème de cassis

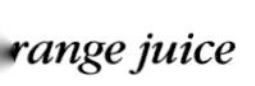

VARIATION

To make a Tequila Sunrise, mix 2 parts tequila with 6 parts orange juice and 2 parts grenadine, then stir gently together.

1 Pour the tequila and the lemon and orange juices into a well-chilled cocktail glass.

2 Using a swizzle stick, mix the ingredients by twisting the stick between the palms of your hands.

3 Drizzle the honey into the center of the cocktail. It will sink and create a layer at the bottom of the glass.

4 Add the crème de cassis, but do not stir. It will create a glowing layer above the honey at the bottom of the glass.

Vunderful

A long, lazy Sunday afternoon tipple, conjured up in the heat of Zimbabwe. Leave the fruits in the gin for as long as possible.

Variation

Use fresh apricots or nectarines and finish either with ginger beer or ginger ale.

Serves 20

Ingredients
14-ounce can lychees
2 peaches, sliced
2½ cups gin

For each serving you will need:
1 measure/1½ tablespoons Pimms
2–3 dashes bitters
5 measures/½ cup chilled tonic water or lemonade
slices of lime, to decorate

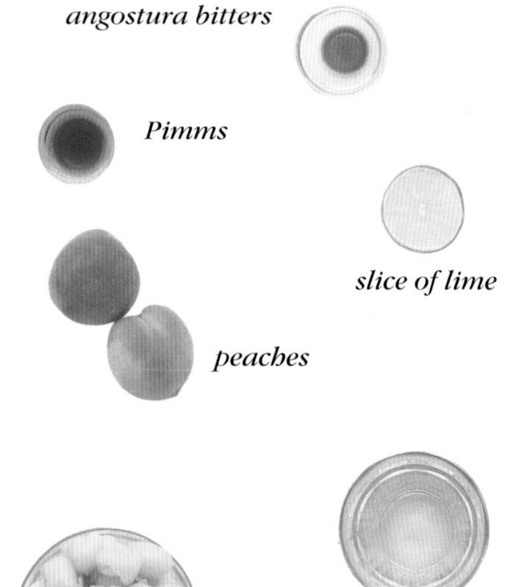

1 Strain the lychees from the syrup and place them in a widemouth jar with the peach slices and the gin. Let sit overnight or up to a month.

2 In a large bar glass or jug, mix for each serving 1 measure/1½ tbsp of the lychee gin with the Pimms and the bitters to taste.

3 Strain into tall tumblers filled with ice cubes.

4 Add chilled tonic water or lemonade to taste.

5 Put some of the drained gin-soaked lychees and peaches into each glass and stir and crush the fruit into the drink using a muddler.

6 Add half a slice of lime to the rim of each glass and serve.

Blue Hawaiian

This drink can be decorated as flamboyantly as Carmen Miranda's headdress with a mixture of fruits and leaves – an eye-catching colorful cocktail that you'll find very drinkable.

Serves 1

INGREDIENTS
- 1 measure/1½ tablespoons blue curaçao
- 1 measure/1½ tablespoons coconut cream
- 2 measures/3 tablespoons light rum
- 2 measures/3 tablespoons pineapple juice
- leaves and wedge of pineapple, slice of prickly pear or orange, a wedge of lime and a maraschino cherry, to decorate

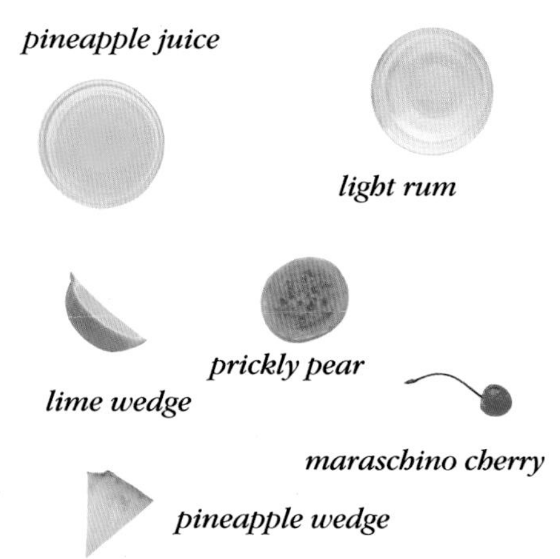

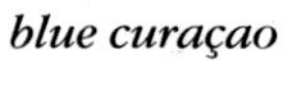

1 Put the curaçao, coconut cream and light rum in a blender. Process very briefly until the color is even.

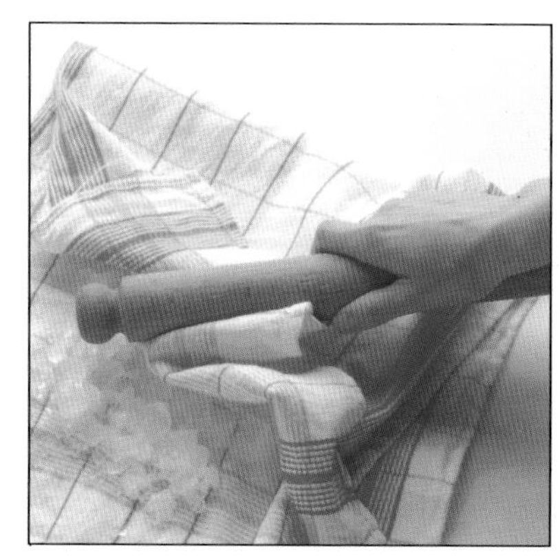

2 Place ice cubes between a dish towel and crush to a fine snow with a wooden hammer or rolling pin.

3 Add the pineapple juice to the blender and process the mixture once more until frothy.

4 Spoon the crushed ice into a large cocktail glass or goblet.

5 Pour the cocktail from the blender over the crushed ice.

6 Decorate with the pineapple leaves and wedge, prickly pear or orange slice, a lime wedge and a maraschino cherry. Serve with a couple of drinking straws.

VARIATION

Pour equal quantities of vodka and blue curaçao over ice. Finish with lemonade for a Blue Lagoon or add equal amounts of gin and curaçao, plus angostura bitters for a Blue Cloak.

Mai Tai

A very refreshing but strong party drink that slides down easily; just before you do!

Serves 1

INGREDIENTS

- 1 measure/1½ tablespoons light rum
- 1 measure/1½ tablespoons dark rum
- 1 measure/1½ tablespoons apricot brandy
- 3 measures/4½ tablespoons orange juice, chilled
- 3 measures/4½ tablespoons pineapple juice, chilled
- 1 measure/1½ tablespoons grenadine

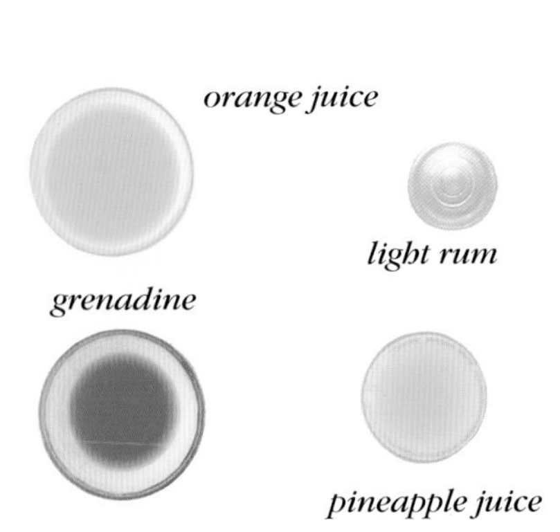

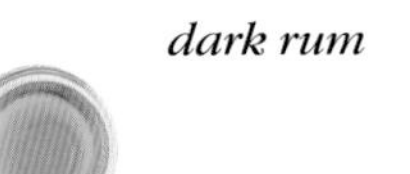

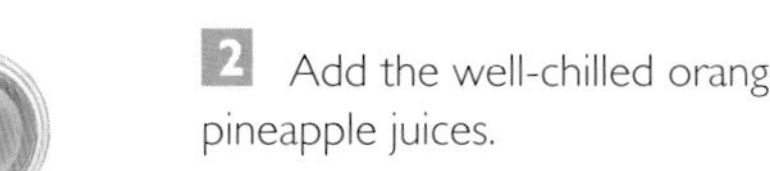

1 Add the light and dark rum and apricot brandy to a cocktail shaker half full of cracked ice.

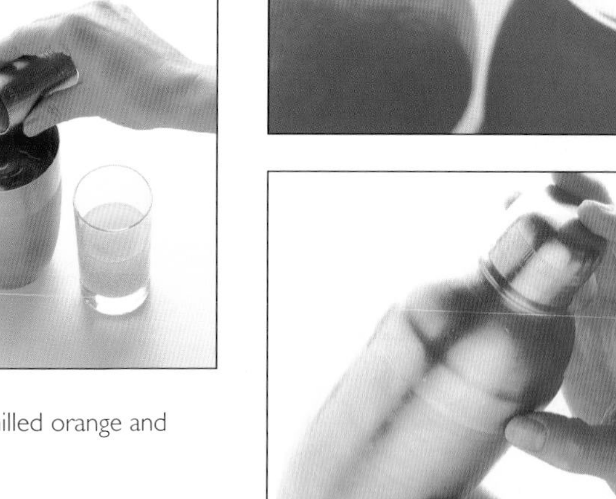

2 Add the well-chilled orange and pineapple juices.

3 Shake well for about 20 seconds, or until the cocktail shaker feels cold. Strain into a tumbler of ice.

4 Slowly pour the grenadine into the glass and it will sink to the bottom of the drink to make a glowing red layer.

VARIATION

Mix bitters, rum and orgeat (almond and orange flower water) syrup or almond essence into 1½ cups orange juice.

Morning Glory Fizz

A good early-morning drink, which should be consumed as soon as it is made, before it loses its flavor and bubbles.

Serves 1

INGREDIENTS

$^{2}/_{3}$ measure/1 tablespoon brandy
$^{1}/_{4}$ measure/1 teaspoon orange curaçao
$^{1}/_{4}$ measure/1 teaspoon fresh lemon juice
1 dash anisette
2 dashes angostura bitters
soda water, to taste
twist of lemon rind, to decorate

1 Pour the brandy, curaçao, lemon juice and anisette into a cocktail shaker containing ice and shake for 20 seconds.

2 Strain the drink into a small chilled cocktail glass.

VARIATION

Shake together an egg white, sugar syrup to taste, the juice of ½ lemon and ½ lime and gin or whiskey instead of the brandy, then add a splash of Chartreuse. Shake well and finish with soda.

3 Add the angostura bitters to taste and finish with the soda water.

4 Using a canelle knife, cut a long thin piece of lemon rind. Curl the lemon rind into a tight coil and add to the drink.

Cider Cup

Cups make an excellent long and refreshing drink for an apéritif or party. Mix up just before serving.

Serves 6

INGREDIENTS
- rind of 1 lemon
- slices of orange
- 5 measures/½ cup pale sherry
- 3 measures/4½ tablespoons brandy or clove brandy
- 3 measures/4½ tablespoons white curaçao
- 2 measures/3 tablespoons amaretto
- 2½ cups good quality hard cider
- cucumber, to decorate

cucumber peel

amaretto

orange slices

lemon rind

hard cider

pale sherry

white curaçao

brandy

1 Partially fill a pitcher with cracked ice and stir in the lemon rind and the orange slices.

2 Add the sherry, brandy, curaçao and amaretto to the ice and stir well to mix.

3 Pour in the cider and stir gently with a long swizzle stick.

4 Using a canelle knife, peel the cucumber around in a continuous piece, to produce a spiral. Serve the cocktail in chilled glasses, decorated with the fruit and a twist of cucumber peel.

VARIATION

Instead of brandy, use Calvados for a richer flavor and add a little maraschino cherry juice to give more color.

Havana Cobbler

An old-fashioned drink that is surprisingly refreshing served in hot weather.

Serves 1

INGREDIENTS
1 tsp sugar syrup
½ measure/2 teaspoons green ginger wine
1 measure/1½ tablespoons Cuban or light rum
1 measure/1½ tablespoons port

light rum

sugar syrup

ginger wine

port

1 Put the sugar syrup and ginger wine in a cocktail shaker half filled with ice. Add the light rum.

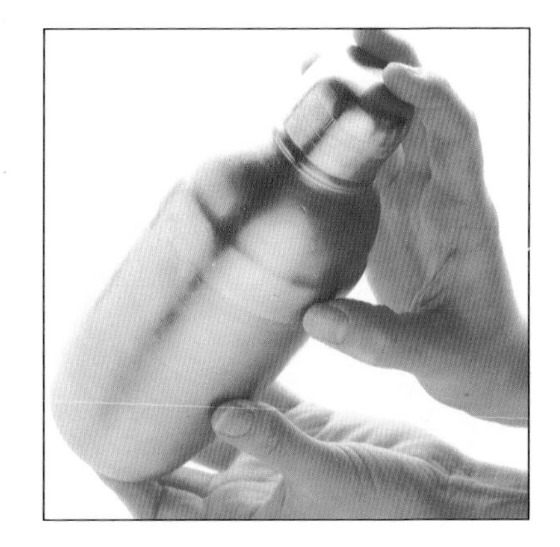

2 Shake together for 20 seconds.

3 Strain the cocktail into a chilled short tumbler.

4 Tilt the glass and slowly pour the port down the side of the glass to form a floating layer on top of the cocktail.

VARIATION

Cobblers can be made with brandy, gin and sherry and even wine or champagne; obviously if you use the latter, remember not to shake it! And omit the port!

Moscow Mule

One of the classic American vodka-based cocktails, which uses a large quantity of angostura bitters for its flavor and color and enough vodka to give the drink a real kick.

Serves 1

INGREDIENTS
2 measures/3 tablespoons vodka
6 dashes angostura bitters
dash of Rose's lime juice
$\frac{1}{2}$ measure/2 teaspoons fresh lime juice
3 measures/$4\frac{1}{2}$ tablespoons ginger beer
slices of lime, to decorate

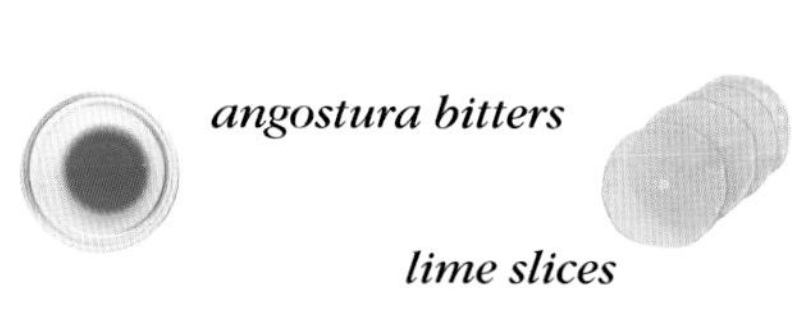

angostura bitters

lime slices

lime juice

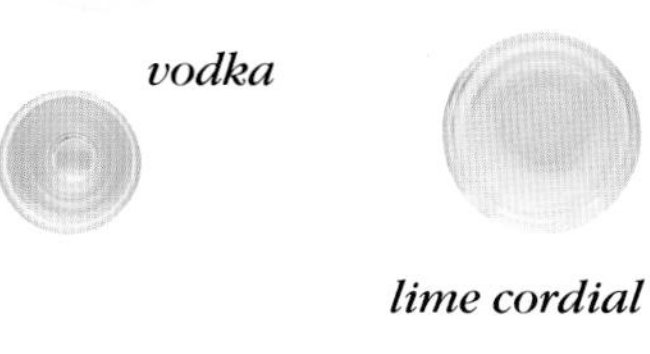

vodka

lime cordial

ginger beer

1 Pour the vodka, bitters, lime cordial and lime juice into a bar glass of ice. Mix together well with a bar spoon.

2 Strain into a tumbler containing a couple of ice cubes.

3 Finish the mixture to taste with ginger beer.

4 Add a few halved slices of lime to the cocktail before serving.

VARIATION

For a Malawi Shandy, mix ice-cold ginger beer with a dash of bitters and finish with soda water. Of course, the vodka does not have to be left out.

Vodka and Kumquat Lemonade

A mild-sounding name for a strong concoction of kumquat and peppercorn-flavored vodka and white curaçao.

VARIATION

Use fruit cordial, with gin or vodka as the base, and finish with soda or tonic water.

Serves 2

INGREDIENTS
- 3 ounces kumquats
- 5 measures/1/2 cup vodka
- 3 black peppercorns, cracked (optional)
- 2/3 measure/1 tablespoon white curaçao or orange syrup
- 2/3 measure/1 tablespoon lemon juice
- 7 measures/ 2/3 cup sparkling mineral or soda water
- slices of kumquats and fresh mint sprigs, to decorate

white curaçao

kumquats

mint sprig

lemon juice

black peppercorns

mineral water

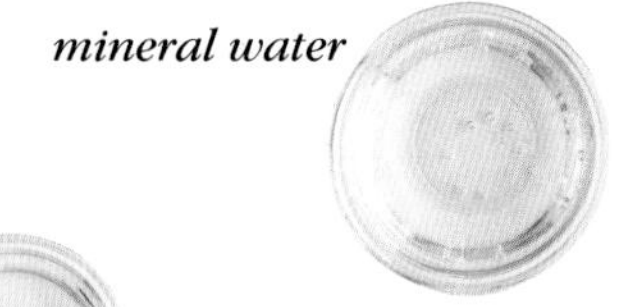

vodka

1 Thickly slice the kumquats and add to the vodka in an airtight jar with the cracked black peppercorns, if using. Set aside for a couple of hours, overnight or for up to a month.

2 Fill a pitcher with cracked ice and then add the curaçao or orange syrup, the lemon juice and the kumquat-flavored vodka with the sliced kumquats.

3 Using a long swizzle stick, stir together well.

4 Add the mineral or soda water and a few fresh mint leaves and gently stir everything together.

5 Pour the drink into chilled glasses of ice.

6 Add slices of kumquats to the glasses and decorate with more mint sprigs.

Horse's Fall

A long drink to serve on a hot summer's day. The addition of strongly flavored tea is a matter of taste and preference.

VARIATION

Substitute Calvados or brandy for the flavored tea for a Horse's Neck.

Serves 1

INGREDIENTS
1 lemon
dash angostura bitters
2 measures/3 tablespoons raspberry, Orange Pekoe or Assam tea, chilled (optional)
1 measure/$1^1/_2$ tablespoons unsweetened apple juice
5 measures/about ½ cup dry ginger ale or lemonade

apple juice

lemon rind

angostura bitters

raspberry tea

dry ginger ale

1 Cut the peel from the lemon in one continuous strip and use it to line and decorate a long cocktail glass. Chill the glass until needed.

2 Add a dash of angostura bitters to the bottom of the glass.

3 Measure the tea, if using, into the cocktail shaker and add the apple juice.

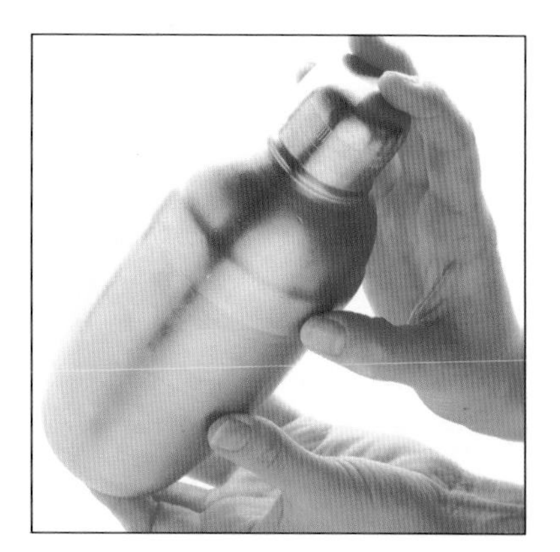

4 Shake everything together for about 20 seconds.

5 Strain into the prepared chilled cocktail glass.

6 Finish with chilled ginger ale or lemonade to taste.

Sunburst

Bursting with freshness and vitamins, this drink is a good early morning pick-me-up.

Serves 2

INGREDIENTS
1 green apple, cored and chopped
3 carrots, peeled and chopped
1 mango, peeled, and pitted
7 measures/⅔ cup freshly squeezed orange juice, chilled
6 strawberries, hulled
slice of orange, to decorate

mango
orange juice
orange slice
carrots
green apple
strawberries

1 Place the apple, carrots and mango in a blender or food processor and process to a pulp.

2 Add the orange juice and strawberries and process again.

3 Strain well through a sieve, pressing out all the juice with the back of a wooden spoon. Discard any pulp left in the sieve.

4 Pour into tumblers filled with ice cubes and serve immediately, decorated with a slice of orange.

VARIATION
Any combination of fruit juice and yogurt can be shaken together. Try natural yogurt with apple, apricot and mango.

Scarlet Lady

This drink could fool a few on the first sip, with its fruity and fresh tones. It could easily pass as an alcoholic wine-based cocktail.

Serves 1

INGREDIENTS
¼ pound cubed Galia, honeydew or watermelon
5 small red seedless grapes
3 measures/4½ tablespoons unsweetened red grape juice
red seedless grapes, sugar-frosted, 1 egg white, lightly beaten and 1 tablespoon sugar, to decorate

egg white

red grape juice

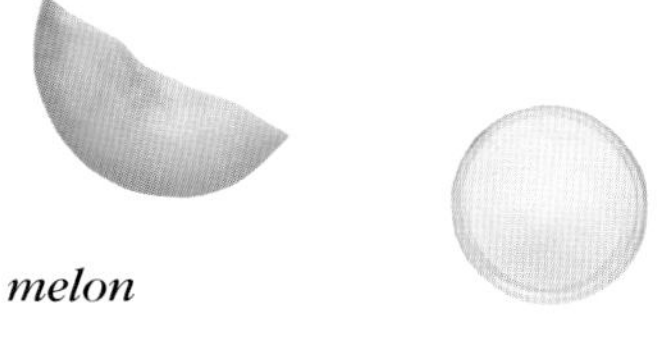

melon

sugar

red grapes

VARIATION
For a longer fizzy drink, finish the melon and grape purée with equal quantities of grape juice and tonic or soda water.

1 Put the melon and grapes in a blender and process until they form a smooth purée.

2 Add the red grape juice and continue to process for another minute.

3 Strain the juice into a bar glass of ice and stir until chilled.

4 Pour into a chilled cocktail glass and decorate with sugar-frosted grapes threaded onto a toothpick.

Virgin Prairie Oyster

A superior pick-me-up and a variation on the Bloody Mary. The tomato base can be drunk without the raw egg yolk if it does not appeal to you. Use only fresh free-range eggs.

Serves 1

INGREDIENTS
¾ cup tomato juice
2 teaspoons Worcestershire sauce
1–2 teaspoons balsamic vinegar
1 egg yolk
cayenne pepper, to taste

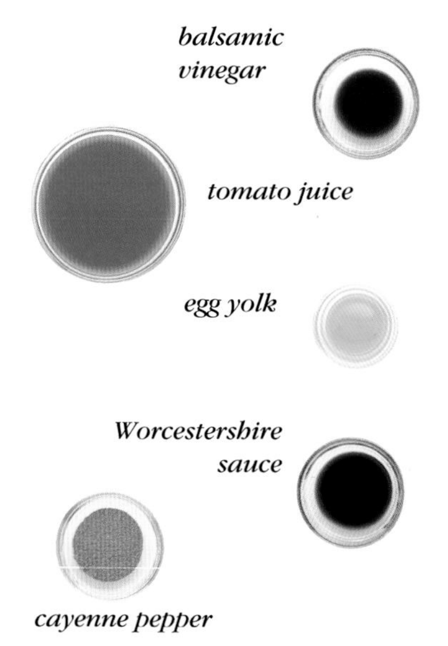

VARIATION

Shake together equal quantities of fresh grapefruit juice and tomato juice with a dash of Worcestershire sauce. Strain into a tall and narrow highball glass.

1 Measure the tomato juice into a large bar glass and stir over plenty of ice until well chilled.

2 Strain into a tall tumbler half filled with ice cubes.

3 Add the Worcestershire sauce and balsamic vinegar to taste and mix with a swizzle stick.

4 Float the egg yolk on top and lightly dust with cayenne pepper.

Fruit and Ginger Ale

An old English mulled drink, served chilled over ice. Of course it can be made with ready-squeezed apple and orange juices, but roasting the fruit with cloves gives a much better flavor.

Serves 4–6

INGREDIENTS
1 cooking apple
1 orange, scrubbed
1 lemon, scrubbed
20 whole cloves
3-inch piece fresh ginger, peeled
1 ounce light brown sugar
1½ cups bitter lemon or non-alcoholic wine
wedges of orange rind and whole cloves, to decorate

ginger

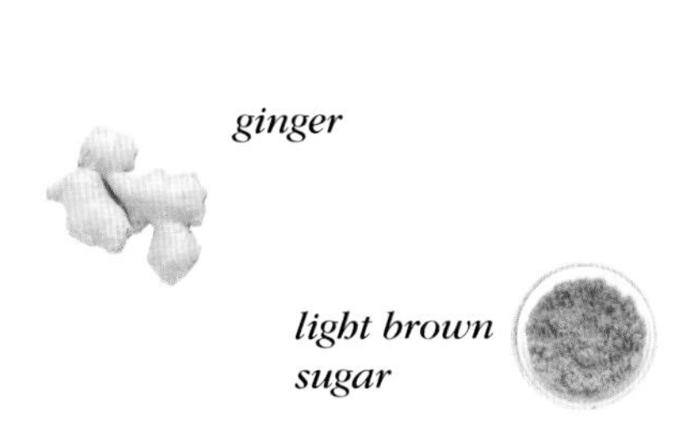

light brown sugar

orange

bitter lemon

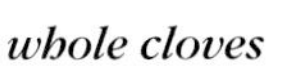

whole cloves

lemon

orange rind

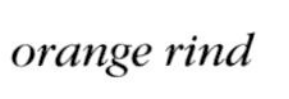

cooking apple

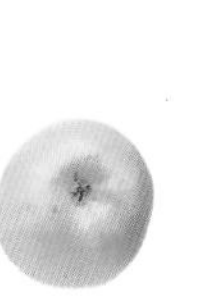

1 Preheat the oven to 400°F. Score the apple around the middle and stud the orange and lemon with the cloves. Bake the fruits in the oven for about 25 minutes, until soft and completely cooked through.

2 Quarter the orange and lemon, mash the apple, discarding the peel and the core. Finely grate the ginger. Place the fruit and ginger in a bowl with the light brown sugar.

3 Add 1¼ cups boiling water. Using a spoon, squeeze the fruit to release more flavor. Cover and let sit for an hour or overnight until cool.

4 Strain into a jug of cracked ice and use a spoon to press out all the juices from the fruit. Add the bitter lemon or non-alcoholic wine to taste. Decorate with orange rind and cloves.

Blushing Piña Colada

This is good with or without the rum. Don't be tempted to put roughly crushed ice into the blender; it will not be as smooth and will ruin the blades. Make sure you crush it well first.

VARIATION

For a classic Piña Colada, use vanilla ic cream and 1 measure light rum. For a Passionate Encounter, blend 2 scoops passionfruit sorbet and coconut milk with a measure each of pineapple and apricot juice.

Serves 2

INGREDIENTS

- 1 banana, peeled and sliced
- 1 thick slice pineapple, peeled
- 3 measures/4½ tablespoons pineapple juice
- 1 scoop strawberry ice cream or sorbet
- 1 measure/1½ tablespoons unsweetened coconut milk
- 2 tablespoons grenadine
- pineapple wedges and maraschino cherries, to decorate

pineapple slice

pineapple juice

grenadine

maraschino cherry

strawberry ice cream

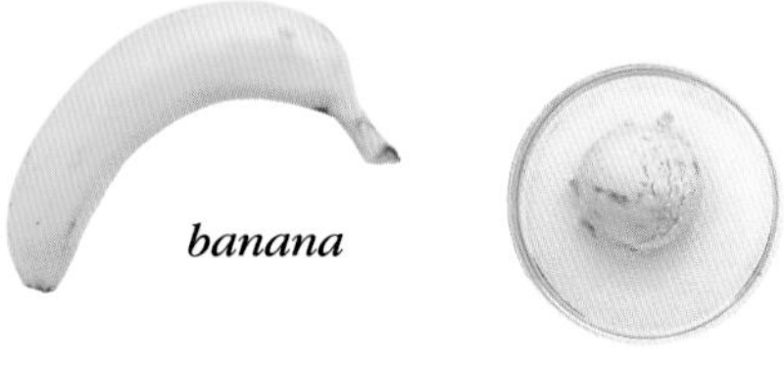

banana

1 Roughly chop the banana. Cut two small wedges from the pineapple for decoration and set aside. Cut up the remainder of the pineapple and add it to the blender with the banana.

2 Add the pineapple juice to the blender and process until the mixture is a smooth purée.

3 Add the strawberry ice cream or sorbet with the coconut milk and a small scoop of finely crushed ice, and process until smooth.

4 Pour into two large, well-chilled cocktail glasses.

5 Pour the grenadine syrup slowly on top of the drink; it will filter down creating a dappled effect.

6 Decorate each glass with a wedge of pineapple and a cherry and serve with drinking straws.

Volunteer

This drink is ideal for a lazy summer afternoon. It's also a fine cocktail to serve the designated driver at a party. It was devised and drunk during a very rough channel crossing in too small a boat!

Serves 1

INGREDIENTS
2 measures/3 tablespoons lime cordial
2– 3 dashes angostura bitters
7 measures/⅔ cup chilled tonic water
decorative ice cubes, to serve
frozen slices of lime, to decorate

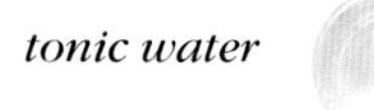

tonic water

angostura bitters

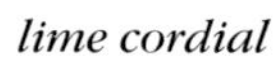

lime cordial

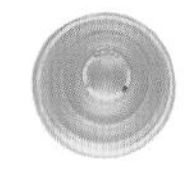

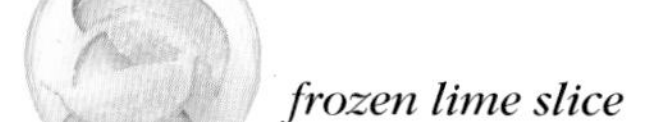

frozen lime slice

1 Place the lime cordial at the bottom of the glass and shake in the angostura bitters to taste.

2 Add a few decorative ice cubes to the glass, if liked.

3 Finish with tonic water and add the frozen lime slices.

VARIATION

Use fresh lime or grapefruit juice and a splash of sugar syrup instead of the lime cordial, and finish with ginger ale.

Steel Works

A thirst quenching drink, which is ideal to serve at any time of the day.

Serves 1

INGREDIENTS

2 measures/3 tablespoons passionfruit cordial
dash angostura bitters
3 measures/4½ tablespoons soda water, chilled
3 measures/4½ tablespoons lemonade, chilled
1 passionfruit (optional)

lemonade

passionfruit cordial

passionfruit

soda water

angostura bitters

1 Pour the passionfruit cordial straight into a long tumbler. Add the angostura bitters to the glass and then add some ice cubes.

2 Finish the drink with the chilled soda water and lemonade and stir briefly together.

3 Cut the passionfruit in half, if using; scoop the seeds and flesh from the fruit and add to the drink. Stir the drink gently before serving.

VARIATION

For a Rock Shandy, pour equal parts of lemonade and soda over bitters or use your favorite variety of the naturally flavored and unsweetened fruit cordials.

Bandrek

A rich and creamy version of the spicy Indonesian drink. Serve warm or chilled. If you like, add a very fresh egg to the syrup and mix in the blender, and you'll have an egg-nog.

VARIATION

Stir ½ measure/2 teaspoons whiskey into the finished drink or add the strained spiced syrup to double-strength black coffee. Process in a blender with a little heavy cream, strain and serve over ice.

Serves 1

INGREDIENTS
- 3 whole cloves
- 3 juniper berries, bruised
- 1 cinnamon stick
- 6 green cardamom pods, bruised
- 4 whole black peppercorns
- 1 sugar cube
- ¾ cup water
- 2 measures/3 tablespoons unsweetened coconut milk
- 3 measures/4½ tablespoons whole milk
- cinnamon sticks and a maraschino cherry, to decorate

coconut milk

cardamom pods

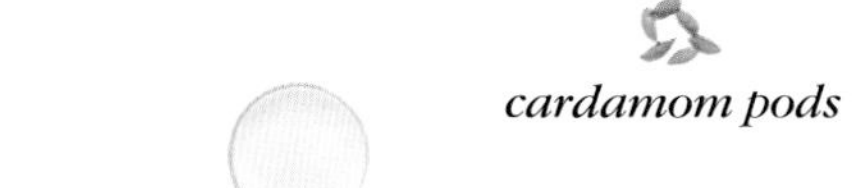

cinnamon sticks

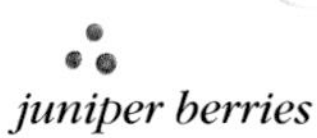

juniper berries

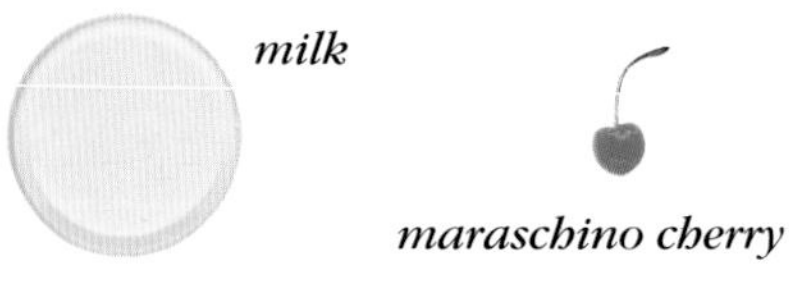

milk

maraschino cherry

sugar cube

1 Put the cloves, juniper berries, cinnamon, cardamom pods, peppercorns and sugar cube in a saucepan. Heat gently to release the aromas and flavors of the spices.

2 Add the water and bring to the boil over medium-high heat.

3 Continue to boil for 10 minutes or until reduced to 2–3 tablespoons of spicy flavored syrup. Remove from the heat and cool.

4 Pour the syrup into a blender with the coconut milk and whole milk and process until smooth.

5 Strain over cracked ice into a stemmed glass.

6 Decorate with cinnamon sticks and a maraschino cherry.

St. Clements

Oranges and lemons create a simple but thirst-quenching drink, which confirms that freshly squeezed fruit has a superior flavor to any of the ready-squeezed versions you can buy.

VARIATION

This same principle can be used to make pineapple, peach, grape and soft fruit juices, but sweeten with sugar syrup. These infusions will keep in the fridge for 2–3 days.

Serves 1

INGREDIENTS
2 oranges
1 lemon
½ ounce sugar, or to taste
5 tablespoons water
orange and lemon slices, to decorate

oranges

sugar

lemon

orange and lemon slices

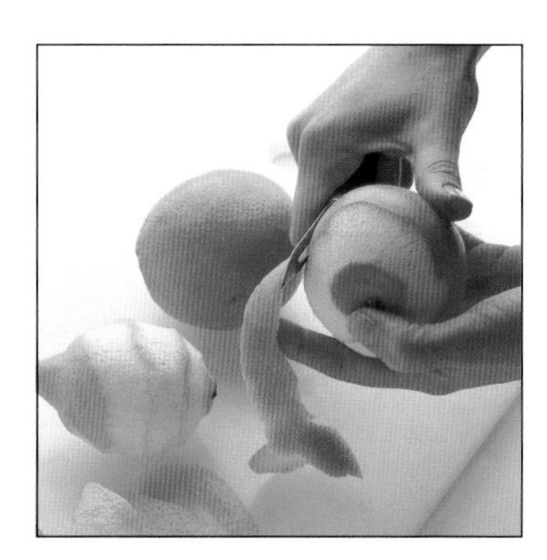

1 Wash the oranges and lemons and then pare the rind off the fruit with a sharp knife, leaving the white pith behind. Remove the pith from the fruit and discard it.

2 Put the orange and lemon rind in a saucepan with the sugar and water. Place over low heat and stir gently until the sugar has dissolved.

3 Remove the pan from the heat and press the orange and lemon rind against the sides of the pan to release all their oils. Cover the pan and let cool. Remove and discard the rind.

4 Purée the oranges and lemon and sweeten the fruit pulp by pouring the cooled citrus syrup over the fruit pulp. Set aside for 2–3 hours to allow the flavors to infuse.

5 Strain the fruit pulp, pressing the solids in the sieve to extract as much of the juice as possible.

6 Pour into a tall glass filled with finely crushed ice and decorate with a slice of orange and lemon.

Dickson's Bloody Mary

This recipe has plenty of character with horseradish, sherry and Tabasco. The true Bloody Mary is simpler.

VARIATION

Use tequila in place of the vodka for a Bloody Maria, use a clam juice and tomato juice mixture for a Bloody Muddle.

Serves 1

INGREDIENTS

- 2 measures/3 tablespoons vodka or chili-flavored vodka
- 1 measure/1½ tablespoons *fino* sherry
- 7 measures/⅔ cup tomato juice
- 1 measure/1½ tablespoons lemon juice
- 2–3 dashes Tabasco sauce
- 2–3 teaspoons Worcestershire sauce
- ½ teaspoon creamed horseradish
- 1 teaspoon celery salt
- salt and ground black pepper
- celery stalk, stuffed green olives and a cherry tomato, to decorate

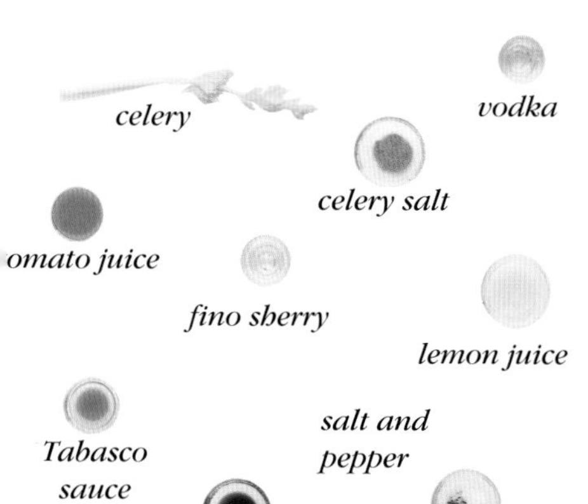

1 Fill a bar glass or pitcher with cracked ice and add the vodka, sherry and tomato juice. Stir well.

2 Add the lemon juice, Tabasco and Worcestershire sauces and the horseradish to taste.

3 Add the celery salt, salt and pepper and stir until the pitcher has frosted and the contents are chilled.

4 Strain into a tall tumbler half filled with a couple of ice cubes.

5 Add a decorative stick of celery as a swizzle stick.

6 Thread a toothpick with olives and a cherry tomato, and place on the rim of the glass, then serve.

Apricot Bellini

This is a version of the famous apéritif served at Harry's Bar in Venice. Instead of the usual peaches and peach brandy, apricot nectar and apricot brandy make this a tempting variation.

Serves 6–8

Ingredients
- 3 apricots
- 2 teaspoons lemon juice
- 2 teaspoons sugar syrup
- 2 measures/3 tablespoons apricot brandy or peach schnapps
- 1 bottle *brut* champagne or dry sparkling wine, chilled

lemon juice

apricots

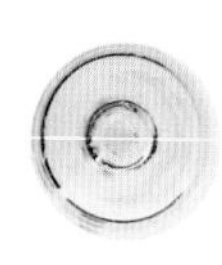

sparkling wine

apricot brandy

sugar syrup

1 Plunge the apricots into boiling water for 2 minutes to loosen the skins.

2 Peel and pit the apricots. Discard the pits and skin.

3 Process the apricot flesh with the lemon juice until you have a smooth purée. Sweeten to taste with sugar syrup, then strain.

4 Add the brandy or peach schnapps to the apricot nectar and stir together.

5 Divide the apricot nectar among chilled champagne flutes.

6 Finish the drinks with chilled champagne or sparkling wine.

Variation

Instead of apricots and apricot brandy, use fresh raspberries and raspberry-infused gin or syrup.

Kir Lethale

The raisins for this cocktail can be soaked overnight in vodka.

Serves 6

INGREDIENTS
- 6 vodka-soaked raisins
- 2 tablespoons vodka or raisin vodka
- 3 measures/$4\frac{1}{2}$ tablespoons crème de cassis
- 1 bottle *brut* champagne or dry sparkling wine, chilled

crème de cassis

vodka-soaked raisins

champagne

VARIATION

For Kir Framboise, use crème de framboise or raspberry syrup and raspberry-flavored vodka.

1 Place a vodka-soaked raisin at the bottom of each glass.

2 Add a teaspoon of vodka or the vodka from the steeped raisins, if using, to each glass.

3 Divide the crème de cassis equally among the glasses.

4 Before serving, finish the drinks with the champagne or sparkling wine.

Brandy Blazer

A warming after-dinner tipple, ideally served with fresh vanilla ice cream or caramelized oranges.

Serves 1

INGREDIENTS
1/2 orange
1 lemon
2 measures/3 tablespoons Cognac
1 sugar cube
1/2 measure/2 teaspoons Kahlúa
orange rind, threaded
on to a cocktail stick, to decorate

lemon

orange rind decoration

Kahlúa

orange

cognac

sugar cube

VARIATION

Pour the hot Cognac and Kahlúa mix into freshly brewed coffee and serve the drink black.

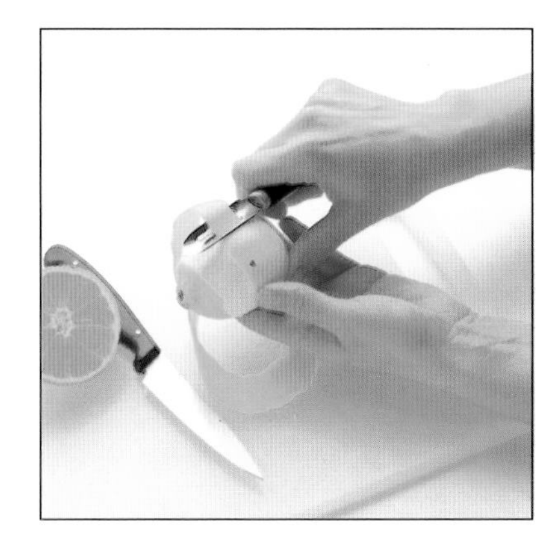

1 Pare the rind from the orange and lemon, removing and discarding as much of the white pith as possible.

2 Put the Cognac, sugar cube, lemon and orange rind in a small pan.

3 Heat gently, then remove from the heat, light a match and pass the flame close to the surface of the liquid. The alcohol will burn with a low, blue flame for about a minute. Blow out the flame.

4 Add the Kahlúa to the pan and strain into a heat-resistant liqueur glass. Decorate with a toothpick threaded with orange rind, then serve warm.

Long Island Iced Tea

A long, potent drink with an intoxicating effect, its strength is well disguised by the cola. For a simpler version, use equal quantities of rum, Cointreau, tequila and lemon juice and top up with cola.

Serves 1

INGREDIENTS

- ½ measure/2 teaspoons light rum
- ½ measure/2 teaspoons vodka
- ½ measure/2 teaspoons gin
- ½ measure/2 teaspoons Grand Marnier or Cointreau
- 1 measure/1½ tablespoons cold Earl Grey tea
- juice of ½ lemon
- cola, chilled, to taste
- slices of lemon and a large fresh mint sprig, to decorate

vodka

lemon juice

cola

lemon slices

mint

1 Fill a bar glass with cracked ice and add the rum, vodka, gin and Grand Marnier or Cointreau.

2 Add the cold Earl Grey tea to the spirits in the bar glass.

3 Stir well for 30 seconds to chill the spirits and the tea.

4 Add lemon juice to taste.

5 Strain into a highball glass filled with ice cubes and lemon.

6 Add chilled cola, to taste, then a fresh mint sprig to use as a swizzle stick.

Mint Julep

One of the oldest cocktails, this originated in the southern States of America. It's the classic accompaniment to the Kentucky Derby.

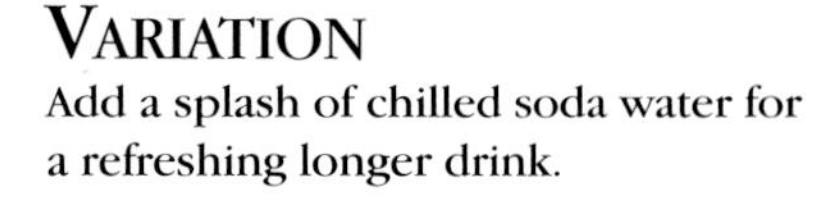

Variation

Add a splash of chilled soda water for a refreshing longer drink.

Serves 1

Ingredients
1 tablespoon sugar
8–10 fresh mint leaves
1 tbsp hot water
2 measures/3 tablespoons bourbon or whiskey

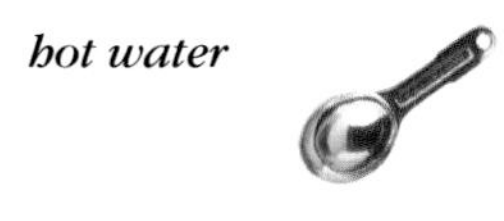

hot water

mint leaves

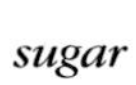

sugar

bourbon

1 Place the sugar in a mortar or in a bar glass. Tear the mint leaves into small pieces and add them to the sugar.

2 Bruise the mint leaves with a pestle or use a muddler to release their flavor and color.

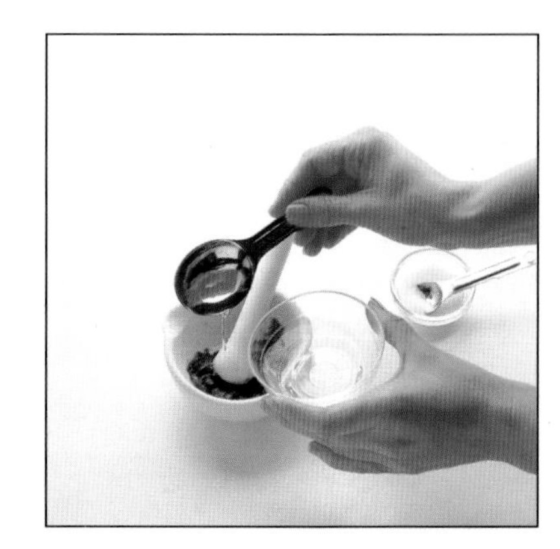

3 Add the hot water to the mint leaves and grind well together.

4 Spoon into a snifter glass or brandy balloon and half fill with crushed ice.

5 Add the bourbon or whiskey to the snifter glass.

6 Stir until the outside of the glass has frosted. Allow to stand for a couple of minutes until the ice melts slightly and dilutes the drink. Serve with straws, if desired.

Frozen Strawberry Daiquiri

A version of the Cuban original, which was made with only local Cuban rum, lime juice and sugar. When out of season, use drained, canned strawberries instead.

VARIATION

Substitute ¼ cup cream for the rum and brandy. Process in the blender and serve as a non-alcoholic daiquiri.

Serves 1

INGREDIENTS
4 strawberries
2 teaspoons fresh lime juice
1 measure/1½ tablespoons brandy or strawberry brandy
1 measure/1½ tablespoons light rum
dash of grenadine
strawberry and a fresh mint sprig, to decorate

strawberries

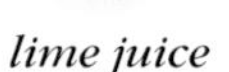

lime juice

light rum

brandy

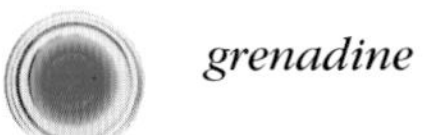

grenadine

mint sprig

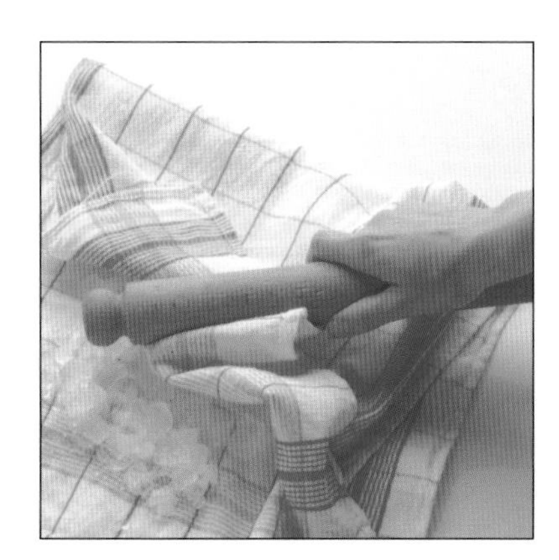

1 Place ice cubes in a clean, folded dish towel and crush to a fine snow using a rolling pin or hammer.

2 Place the strawberries with the lime juice and brandy in a blender and process to a purée.

3 Add the light rum, grenadine and half a glass of finely crushed ice to the blender and process once more, to a smooth slush.

4 Pour the mixture into a well-chilled cocktail glass.

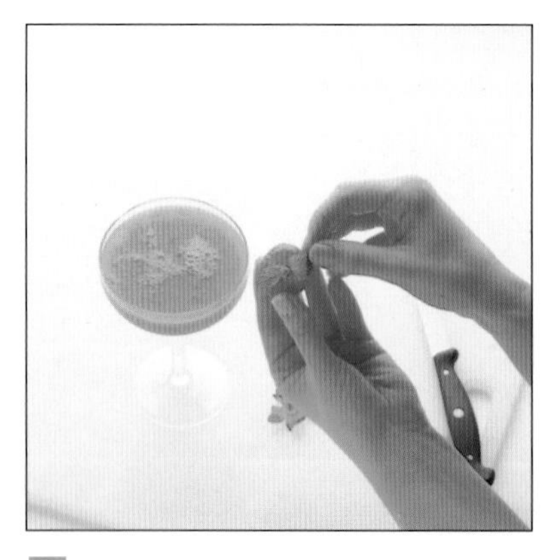

5 To decorate, remove the hull from the strawberry and replace with a small sprig of fresh mint.

6 Make a cut in the side of the strawberry and attach to the rim of the glass. Serve with a short straw, if liked.

Wilga Hill Boomerang

This sundowner is mixed in a large bar glass half filled with ice cubes, and is served super cold.

Serves 1

INGREDIENTS
1 measure/$1^1/_2$ tablespoons gin
$^1/_4$ measure/1 teaspoon dry vermouth
$^1/_4$ measure/1 teaspoon sweet vermouth
1 measure/$1^1/_2$ tablespoons apple juice
dash angostura bitters
2 dashes maraschino cherry juice
strip of orange rind and a maraschino cherry, to decorate

1 Pour the gin, dry and sweet vermouths and apple juice into a bar glass half filled with ice, and stir until the outside of the glass has frosted.

2 Add the angostura bitters and maraschino juice to the bottom of a cocktail glass and add ice cubes.

3 Strain the cocktail into a shorts tumbler.

4 Add the strip of orange rind and a maraschino cherry and serve.

VARIATION

Omit the apple juice and serve over the rocks or, if preferred, substitute bourbon or Southern Comfort for the gin.

Golden Start

A delicious and very drinkable mix of Galliano, orange, pineapple and cream of coconut.

Serves 1

INGREDIENTS
- 2 measures/3 tablespoons Galliano
- 1 measure/1½ tablespoons orange juice, chilled
- 1 measure/1½ tablespoons pineapple juice, chilled
- 1 measure/1½ tablespoons white or orange curaçao
- 1 measure/1½ tablespoons cream of coconut
- 2 tablespoons pineapple juice and 1 ounce sugar, to decorate

white curaçao

Galliano

sugar

orange juice

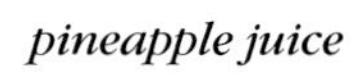

pineapple juice

cream of coconut

1 Put the Galliano, orange and pineapple juices and curaçao in a blender and process together.

2 Add the cream of coconut with a tablespoon of fine ice snow and process until smooth and frothy.

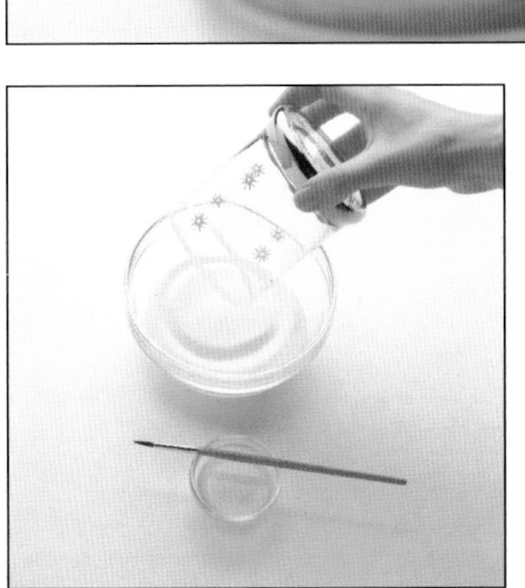

3 Rub the rim of the cocktail glass with pineapple juice and invert the glass into a saucer of sugar to frost the rim.

4 Pour the cocktail into the prepared glass while still frothy.

VARIATION

For an extra tropical twist, substitute light crème de cacao for the curaçao.

Sea Dog

A long whiskey drink with a citrus twist. For a sweeter drink, add another sugar cube; if including Drambuie, use only one.

Variation

Use gin in place of the whiskey and Pimms in place of the Benedictine.

Serves 1

Ingredients
- 1–2 sugar cubes
- 2 dashes angostura bitters
- 2 oranges wedges
- 2 lemon wedges
- $^{2}/_{3}$ measure/1 tablespoon whiskey or Drambuie
- 1 measure/$1^{1}/_{2}$ tablespoons Benedictine
- 2 measures/3 tablespoons soda water, chilled, or to taste
- maraschino cherry, to decorate

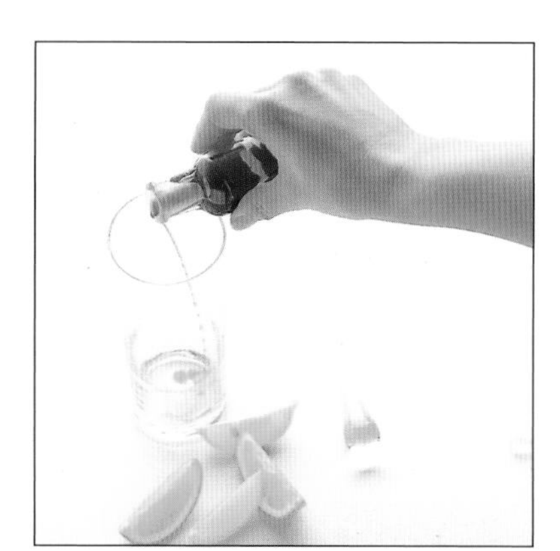

1 Put the sugar cube at the bottom of a Collins glass, add the bitters and allow to soak into the sugar cube.

2 Add the orange and lemon wedges and, using a muddler, press the juices from the fruit.

3 Fill the glass with cracked ice.

4 Add the whiskey and the Benedictine and mix together well with a swizzle stick for 20 seconds.

5 Add chilled soda water to taste.

6 Serve with the muddler, so that more juice can be pressed from the fruit, according to personal taste; decorate with a maraschino cherry.

Harvey Wallbanger

The next step up from a Screwdriver – with a dash of Galliano. Those who prefer a stronger cocktail should add an extra measure of vodka.

VARIATION

Combine the orange juice and vodka with a splash of ginger wine, pour into a glass and slowly pour the Galliano on top.

Serves 1

INGREDIENTS

1 measure/1½ tablespoons vodka
⅔ measure/1 tablespoon Galliano
7 measures/⅔ cup orange juice
½ small orange, to decorate

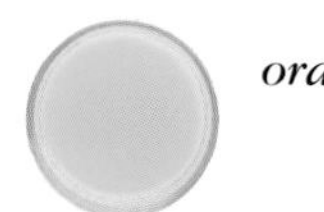

orange juice

Galliano

orange

vodka

1 Pour the vodka, Galliano and orange juice into a bar glass of ice.

2 Mix the cocktail and ice for 30 seconds to chill it well.

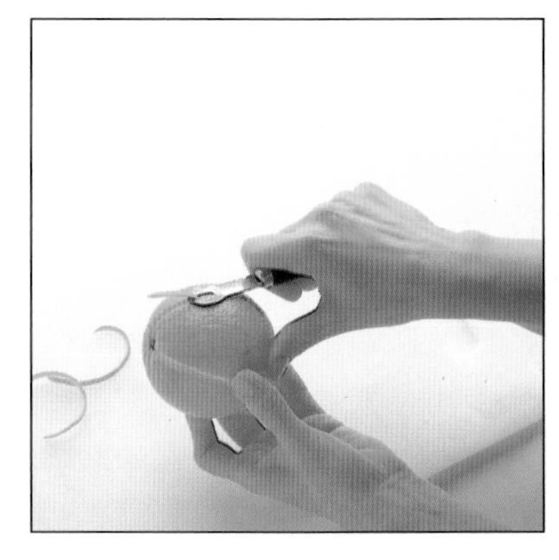

3 Using a canelle knife, take a series of strips of rind off the orange, running from the top to the bottom of the fruit.

4 Use a small, sharp knife to cut the orange evenly and thinly into slices.

5 Cut the orange slices in half and wedge them between cracked ice in a highball glass.

6 Strain the chilled cocktail into the prepared glass.

Apple Sour

For those with concerns about eating raw egg, this variation on a Brandy Sour can be made without the egg white. Applejack or apple schnapps also works well, in place of the Calvados.

Serves 1

INGREDIENTS

1 measure/$1\frac{1}{2}$ tablespoons Calvados
$\frac{2}{3}$ measure/1 tablespoon lemon juice
1 teaspoon sugar
1 dash angostura bitters
1 egg white
red and green apple slices and fresh lemon juice, to decorate

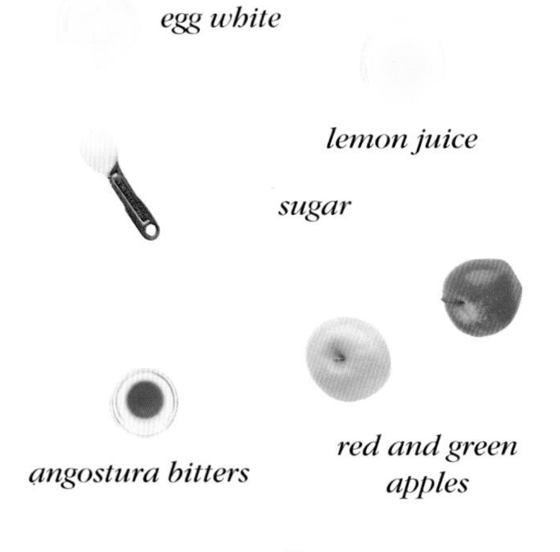

1 Add the Calvados, lemon juice and sugar into a shaker of ice, with the angostura bitters and egg white.

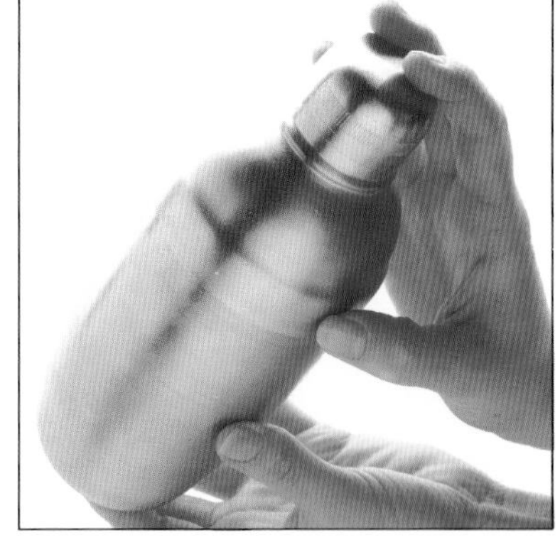

2 Shake together for 30 seconds.

3 Strain the cocktail into a tumbler of cracked ice.

4 Dip the red and green apple slices in lemon juice. Decorate the cocktail with the apple slices threaded onto a bamboo skewer.

VARIATION

Sours can also be made with Amaretto or tequila; add a splash of raspberry syrup or port to the glass just before serving.

East India

This short and elegant drink can be served as an apéritif, dressed with a twist of lime rind and a maraschino cherry.

Serves 1

INGREDIENTS
- 2/3 measure/1 tablespoon brandy
- 2 dashes white curaçao
- 2 dashes pineapple juice
- 2 dashes angostura bitters
- 1 lime and a maraschino cherry, to decorate

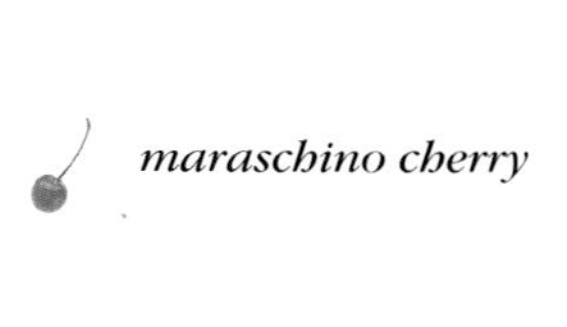

maraschino cherry

lime

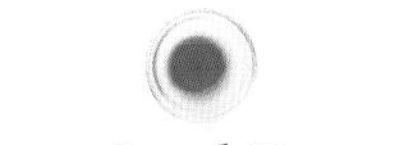

angostura bitters

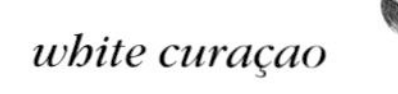

white curaçao

brandy

pineapple juice

1 Put the brandy, curaçao, pineapple juice and bitters into a bar glass of ice.

2 Stir the cocktail well for about 20 seconds until chilled and strain into a squat tumbler over the rocks.

3 Using a canelle knife, remove a piece of rind from a lime.

4 Tightly twist into a coil, hold for a few seconds, and add to the drink with a maraschino cherry.

VARIATION

Mix equal quantities of dry vermouth and dry sherry with angostura bitters and serve on the rocks.

Planters Punch

This long, refreshing, old colonial drink originates from the sugar plantations that are dotted throughout the West Indies.

Serves 1

INGREDIENTS
1 measure/1½ tablespoons fresh lime juice
1 measure/1½ tablespoons orange juice (optional)
2 measures/3 tablespoons dark rum
2 teaspoons grenadine
1 dash angostura bitters
soda water or lemonade, chilled
peach slices and a Cape gooseberry, to decorate

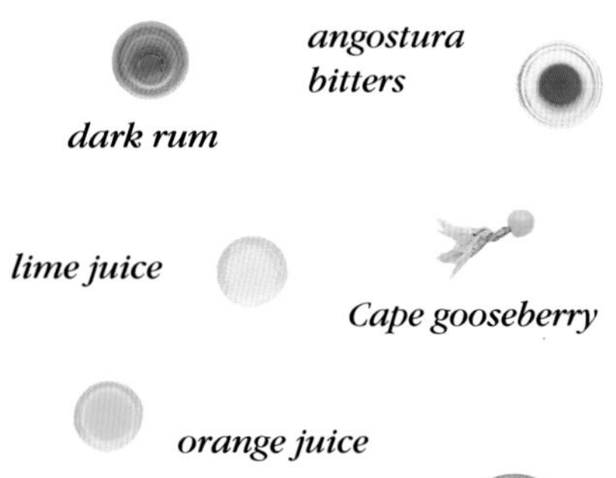

peach

soda water

1 Squeeze the lime and orange juices and add to a bar glass of ice.

2 Add the dark rum and the grenadine and mix together for about 20 seconds.

3 Add a dash of bitters to the bottom of a tumbler of decorative ice cubes.

4 Strain the rum and grenadine mixture into the chilled tumbler.

5 Finish with plenty of chilled soda water or lemonade.

6 Decorate with peach slices and a Cape gooseberry.

VARIATION

Add 1 measure/1½ tablespoons cold Assam tea, for a different tang.

Singapore Sling

The origins of this old-fashioned thirst quencher lie far away to the east.

VARIATION
Substitute Benedictine for the Cointreau for a Straits Sling. Add ginger beer instead of soda water for a Raffles Bar Sling.

Serves 1

INGREDIENTS
2 measures/3 tablespoons gin
juice of 1 lemon
1 teaspoon sugar
soda water, chilled
$^{2}/_{3}$ measure/1 tablespoon Cointreau
$^{2}/_{3}$ measure/1 tablespoon cherry brandy
1 lemon and 1 black cherry, to decorate

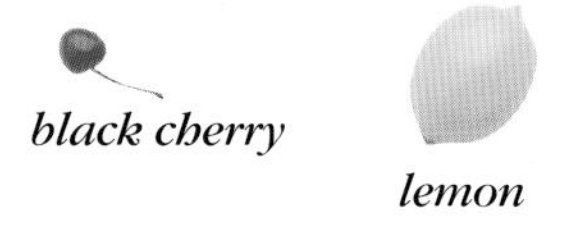

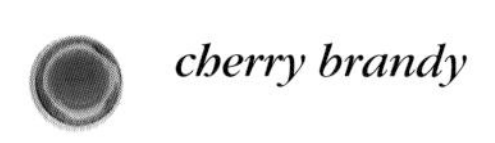

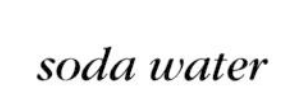

1 Pour the gin into a bar glass of ice and mix with the lemon juice and sugar.

2 Strain the cocktail into a tumbler full of cracked ice.

3 Finish the cocktail with chilled soda water to taste.

4 Add the Cointreau and the cherry brandy, but do not stir.

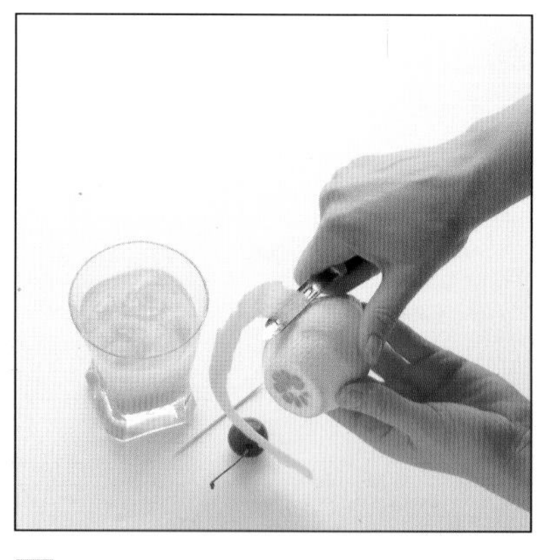

5 To decorate, use a vegetable peeler or sharp knife to cut a long piece of rind round the lemon.

6 Place the lemon rind in the glass. Thread the cherry onto two toothpicks and add to the rim of the glass.

Kew Pimms

A very drinkable concoction of sweet vermouth, curaçao, vodka, gin and cherry brandy served over summer fruit.

Variation

For a longer drink, finish with champagne, sparkling wine or tonic water.

Serves 1

Ingredients
- 1 measure/1½ tablespoons sweet vermouth
- 1 measure/1½ tablespoons orange curaçao
- ⅔ measure/1 tablespoon vodka
- ⅔ measure/1 tablespoon gin
- ⅔ measure/1 tablespoon cherry brandy
- assorted soft summer fruits
- 1–2 dashes angostura bitters
- 2 measures/3 tablespoons American dry ginger ale, chilled
- 2 measures/3 tablespoons lemonade, chilled
- 1 lemon, to decorate
- fresh lemon balm or mint leaves, to decorate

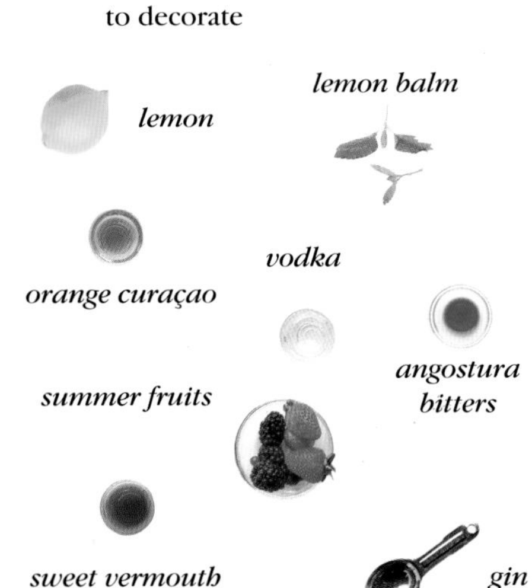

1 Measure the vermouth, curaçao, vodka, gin and cherry brandy into a bar glass of ice and stir well to chill.

2 Strain into a tall highball glass full of ice cubes and the summer fruits.

3 Add the bitters and then pour in equal quantities of chilled ginger ale and lemonade to taste.

4 To make lemon triangles, pare a thin piece of lemon rind from the lemon.

5 Cut the rind into a rectangle and cut a slit three-quarters of the way across the lemon rind. Turn the rectangle and repeat from the other side.

6 Twist to form a triangle, crossing the ends to secure them. Add to the drink with lemon balm or mint leaves.